SERIES EDITOR: LEE JOHNS

MEN-AT-ARMS 339

THE KING'S GERMAN LEGION (2) 1812-1816

TEXT AND COLOUR PLATES BY
MIKE CHAPPELL

OSPREY
MILITARY

Ac

First published in 2000 by Osprey Publishing,
Elms Court, Chapel Way, Botley, Oxford OX2 9LP, UK
Email: info@ospreypublishing.com

ISBN 1 85532 997 2

Editor: Martin Windrow
Design: Alan Hamp
Origination by Grasmere Digital Imaging, Leeds, UK
Printed in China through World Print Ltd

00 01 02 03 04 10 9 8 7 6 5 4 3 2 1

FOR A CATALOGUE OF ALL TITLES PUBLISHED BY OSPREY MILITARY,
AUTOMOTIVE AND AVIATION PLEASE WRITE TO:
The Marketing Manager, Osprey Publishing Ltd, PO Box 140,
Wellingborough, Northants NN8 4ZA, United Kingdom
Email: info@OspreyDirect.co.uk

The Marketing Manager, Osprey Direct USA, PO Box 130,
Sterling Heights, MI 48311-0310, USA
Email: info@OspreyDirectUSA.com

Visit Osprey at www.ospreypublishing.com

Author's Note

The author wishes to thank Dr Mijndert Bertram of the Bomann
Museum, Celle, Germany, for his help in the preparation of this title;
Frau Sabine Bell for her help with translation; the staff of the Prince
Consort's Library, Aldershot; the staff of the Historisches Museum,
Hannover; Mr Harry Robertson; and Peter Harrington of the Anne
S.K.Brown Military Collection, Brown University, Rhode Island, USA

Note that an apparent inconsistency in spelling is due to the
difference between English and German forms – respectively
'Hanover' and 'Hannover'. Throughout the text we follow period
practice in using English forms of the Christian names of
Hanoverian officers, e.g. Charles rather than Karl von Alten, etc.

TITLE PAGE ILLUSTRATION **Side drum of 2nd Line Battalion,
KGL, with 1796 pattern heavy cavalry sword and 1796
pattern light cavalry sabre. (Author's drawing)**

OPPOSITE **An officer of the 1st Hussars, KGL, c.1815 – one
of a series of line-and-wash drawings by Capt Count
Castell, an officer of the 3rd Hanoverian Hussars, made at
some time in the 1820s or early 1830s. Amongst the
earliest representations of the Legion, and drawn while the
details were fairly fresh in the memories of those who
served, they are therefore the most important source of
KGL uniform information.**

**The dark blue dolman is shown with the red facings of the
1st Hussars, the overalls with gold stripes; the dolman and
pelisse have lavish gold lace and braid trim, and the latter is
edged with black fur; the barrel-sash is red and gold. The
dark brown fur cap has a red bag, gold cords and a white-
over-red plume. (Author's collection)**

THE KING'S GERMAN LEGION (2) 1812-1816

1812: THE TURNING OF THE TIDE

BY THE YEAR 1812 Napoleon Bonaparte, Emperor of the French, had all but succeeded in his aims to bend the countries of Europe to his declared will, and to have them 'melted into one nation' with Paris as its capital. He had by then pushed out the frontiers of France and surrounded them with satellite kingdoms, usually with members of his family sitting on their thrones. He had forced the greater part of Europe that he now controlled to adopt his legal 'Code Napoléon' and his educational reforms; he sought – with variable success – to deny these countries' trade to British merchants and their ports to British shipping; and he exacted from them manpower for his armies and money for his exchequer. To the east Austria, Prussia and Russia ostensibly retained their independence, but had been forced into effective neutrality by their memories of shattering defeats at the hands of the emperor at Austerlitz, Jena and Friedland.

Only in Spain had there been a national uprising against occupation by the French. There – aided by the British, and by a liberated Portugal which had thrown in its lot with Britain – battered Spanish armies continued to wage regional campaigns, supported by the Spanish people in a guerrilla war of frightful savagery – repaid in full measure by the French. Britain remained Napoleon's constant enemy, dominating the seas with her navy, using her great wealth to fund and arm other nations in their opposition to the emperor, and conducting military operations in the Peninsula and the Mediterranean.

A growing quarrel between Napoleon and Czar Alexander of Russia spilled over into war in June 1812 when the emperor marched against his adversary at the head of his Grande Armée, a force totalling 675,000 men from France and her satellites. This decision was to mark a turning point in the fortunes of Napoleon, who was now committed to war on two fronts – Russia and Spain. After hard fighting he reached Moscow in September, but before the year was out his army had been forced into a disastrous retreat, losing at least 380,000 men in the process. In October a republican coup was attempted in Paris, whilst in Spain Wellington's armies were gaining the upper hand. In the months to come the nations of Europe were to band together in a coalition against Napoleon and invade France. In April 1814 he was forced to abdicate, and went into his first exile on the Mediterranean island of Elba.

* * *

In the forefront of the fight against Napoleon were the men of the King's German Legion, whose early history is told in the accompanying Men-at-

Arms 338, *The King's German Legion (1) 1803-1812*. Driven from their homeland of Hanover after its invasion by the French in 1803, they had journeyed to England at the request of King George III (who was also their sovereign as the Elector of Hanover), and there formed a military force of all arms.

By late 1812 the KGL comprised two regiments of dragoons, three regiments of hussars, two battalions of Light infantry, eight battalions of Line infantry, four batteries of foot artillery, two batteries of horse artillery, a garrison company and a depot company. There were a number of engineer officers; and in 1813 a Foreign Veteran Battalion would be formed from the worn-out men of the other units and the depot and garrison companies. Units were deployed as follows:

United Kingdom 1st and 2nd Batteries of Horse Artillery; 3rd Hussars (less a detachment in the Peninsula), and the depot.
Peninsula 1st, 2nd and 4th Foot Batteries; 1st and 2nd Dragoons; 1st and 2nd Hussars; 1st and 2nd Light Battalions; 1st, 2nd and 5th Line Battalions.
Peninsula (Catalonia) 4th and 6th Line Battalions.
Portugal Independent Garrison Company, KGL.
Sicily/Malta 3rd Foot Battery; 3rd, 7th and 8th Line Battalions (whose grenadier and light companies also carried out operations in Catalonia).

1812: Retreat after victory

The first part of this history concluded with Wellington's victory at Salamanca on 22 July 1812, and the triumph of the two dragoon regiments of the KGL at Garcia Hernandez on the following day when they routed the infantry of the French rearguard, breaking their squares in the process. When Wellington's forces entered Madrid on 12 August 1812 the dragoons of the Legion were given the place of honour at their head.

They came to the parade straight from the battlefield, for only the previous day they had fought an action against enemy cavalry, losing their brigade commander, six other officers and 48 men. The enemy – the Lanciers de Berg and Italian dragoons – had surprised the dragoons of the KGL at rest, but with the support of the 1st Light Battalion they were able to rally and fight back. The KGL were soon to encounter their fellow Germans of the Lanciers de Berg yet again.

On 27 August the city of Seville was taken from its French garrison, the conduct of a detachment of the KGL 2nd Hussars being mentioned in despatches.

Leaving a holding force in Madrid, Wellington advanced north against the French-held fortress of Burgos, which he invested on 19 September 1812. Burgos was a major depot for the enemy, dominating the main highway to France. Its capture was crucial, and although Wellington had no proper siege train to breach its walls, attempts were made to storm the defences on 22 and 29 September. These met with no success, and set a pattern which continued until 20 October, when the siege was given up. It had cost the British over 2,000 casualties, 368 of which were from the King's German Legion.

In his despatches Wellington singled out the gallantry of the men of the Legion in the final assault for particular praise. The behaviour of one

Castell drawing of an officer of the 2nd Hussars, c.1815. The uniform differs considerably from that of the officer of the 1st Hussars, especially in the brown fur shako and gold-striped light grey overalls. Note the white facings of the 2nd Hussars at collar and cuffs, the pale grey fur edging to the pelisse, red-and-gold pouch belt, red cap bag, white-over-red cap plume, and rich decoration of gold lace and braid. The pelisse lining is shown as red. Sabres were of the 1796 pattern but of a higher quality than those of the rank-and-file. Castell shows sword belts as black leather for officers, with three suspension straps for the sabretasche. (Author's collection)

man, Private Christian Hallego of the 2nd Line Battalion, was eventually rewarded with the Guelphic Medal for his bravery in the trenches before Burgos and his conduct as a member of the 'forlorn hope' storming party on 18 October. (He was to distinguish himself yet again at the battle of Waterloo.)

With enemy forces concentrating in their rear, Wellington's army now began the long march back to Portugal and safety. They were followed by a French force of over 40,000, who caught up with the British rearguard on 23 October at a place called Venta del Pozo. Driving in the British cavalry screen, the cavalry of the French advance guard were ambushed by the rifle fire of the 2nd Light Battalion KGL and forced to retire. They came on again, and the 2nd Light fell back to the positions of the 1st Light Battalion, both battalions forming square to receive cavalry. In this formation they conducted a fighting withdrawal over several miles, supported by the Legion's 1st and 2nd Dragoons and the 1st Hussars. The punishing musketry of the Light battalions inflicted heavy casualties on the French cavalry, which again included the Lanciers de Berg. This model rearguard action was witnessed by Wellington, who sent his thanks and a double rum ration to the German light infantrymen. (Both battalions were later granted the battle honour of 'Venta del Pozo', which was still being worn on the caps of the 10th Hanoverian Jäger Battalion in 1914, alongside the honours 'Peninsula' and 'Waterloo' – see page 39.)

Madrid was evacuated (after the King's German Artillery had destroyed the weapons, ammunition and stores seized when the city had fallen to the British), and Wellington's forces retired across the border into Portugal in miserable weather conditions which deteriorated as the rain turned to snow. Rations went astray and discipline broke down as hungry men left the columns in search of food, liquor and loot. By the time safety was reached Wellington had lost 5,000 men and his forces were badly in need of rest, refitting and reinforcement.

The failure to take Burgos and the ignominious retreat to Portugal diminished the glory of Salamanca, and in England criticism was voiced at Wellington's conduct of the war (which nonetheless did not hinder his elevation to marquis). But events were turning in the favour of Britain and her allies. In the east Napoleon's troops were perishing in tens of thousands as the Russian winter gripped them. In southern Spain the French had abandoned their siege of Cadiz; and throughout the Peninsula the Spanish guerrilla bands fell upon the French at every opportunity, cutting the enemy's communications, butchering supply convoys, and bringing Wellington's intelligence officers valuable information.

Castell line-and-wash drawing of an officer of the 3rd Hussars, KGL, c.1815; this was the unit which avenged the slaughter of Col von Ompteda and the 5th Line Bn at Waterloo. The artist shows a brown fur shako with a red bag and a white-over-red plume, yellow facings and silver lace and braid to his dolman, pelisse and overalls. His pouch belt is also of silver lace on yellow leather, but his cap cords and sash barrels are gold. The pose displays the scarlet lining of the pelisse, which is edged with brown fur. (Author's collection)

RIGHT **Another in the Castell series shows an officer of the 1st Light Dragoons, c.1815 – after 'Bock's Heavy Germans' of Garcia Fernandez fame had been converted to light dragoons and adopted the 1812 uniform of that branch. All the lace on his uniform is gold, including that on his red leather pouch belt and sword belt. His jacket is dark blue with red facings and his overalls are grey. His 1796 pattern light cavalry sabre has a gold and crimson sword knot. The chin-scales of his shako are shown fastened above the peak. (Author's collection)**

FAR RIGHT **An officer of the 1st Light Battalion, c.1815. With his black shako, rifle-green jacket and grey overalls Castell's subject resembles an officer of a British rifle regiment; but details of his uniform mark him out as belonging to the KGL, and to the 1st Light in particular. The carrot shape of the black plume in his cap is one of these, and the two rows of buttons on his jacket are another. Note his silver 'light infantry' pattern wings, his crimson whip-sash, his black leather waistbelt and pouch belt, and his 1803 pattern flank company officer's sword. See also Plate C1. (Author's collection)**

1813: The campaigns in northern Germany

By 1813 the scale of the disaster which had befallen Napoleon in Russia was clear to all. As the Russian armies pushed westward and Napoleon struggled to organise fresh armies to face them while still defending the other frontiers of his empire, his allies began to revise their allegiances. In February the King of Prussia joined forces with the Czar. The Hanseatic states and Sweden rallied to the Allied cause, while Hanover was among a number of German states which declared their independence. For the time being Austria maintained a wary neutrality, but this was not to last. From April until June a series of manoeuvres and battles took place in which Napoleon defeated the Allies at Lützen and Bautzen before an armistice was negotiated and came into effect. After a two-month pause the fighting resumed, this time with Austria arrayed with the other Allied powers against the French; and in October Napoleon was defeated at Leipzig in what came to be called 'the Battle of the Nations'. By the end of 1813 he was at bay on the frontiers of France itself.

The King's German Legion's involvement in these great events was limited to a side-show in northern Germany. There, by March 1813 the French had fallen back to the line of the river Elbe, the Russians had

Castell drawing of a private soldier of the 1st Light Bn, c.1815, showing his subject in black shako and equipment, rifle-green jacket and grey trousers. He also shows a distinctive black cap tuft rising from a ball-shaped base, and a single row of buttons to his jacket. The jacket had black wing-like rolls at the point of the shoulder and was cut away to short tails at the back – cf.Plates D & E, MAA 338. (Author's collection)

entered Berlin and linked up with the Prussians, and the French had evacuated Hamburg. An Allied corps was forming on the lower Elbe under the Prince Royal of Sweden and the Hanoverian General Wallmoden. (Wallmoden was the eldest son of the field-marshal who had commanded the Hanoverian forces in 1803, and had served in both Austrian and Russian service. He now held a British commission as a lieutenant-general, and in 1814 was to be appointed colonel-commandant of the 1st Light Dragoons of the King's German Legion.) The corps was made up of Russian formations and units of the Hanseatic Legion, Hanoverian units, Mecklenburgh units, a Prussian unit and a Dessau unit, totalling 5,600 infantry and 6,000 cavalry. Nearly all of these were new levies.

Britain had agreed to arm, clothe and equip a force of 10,000 released Russian prisoners-of-war to be called 'the Russian German Legion', and to ship to the Baltic further military stores and £2,000,000 sterling for the maintenance of the force (a colossal sum in those days). To bolster the force a detachment of the King's German Legion was assembled and set sail for Hamburg in April. It consisted of 400 men of the two Light Battalions and the 1st, 2nd and 5th Line Battalions, a detachment of the 1st Hussars, and six guns of the King's German Artillery.

The task of this force was to support Hamburg, to secure the line of the Elbe, and to cover the rear of the Russians operating near Berlin. It soon came under attack from French forces under Marshal Davout, who sought to cross the river and to retake Hamburg, which he achieved on 31 May. The armistice brought operations to an end from 4 June, and shortly afterwards a second detachment of the KGL joined the Allied force; this comprised LtCol Hugh Halkett of the 7th Line Battalion, who was to command a brigade of Hanoverian levies, and a party of officers, non-commissioned officers and men of the Legion to lead and train them. There was also a detachment of the 2nd Dragoons. While the armistice lasted every opportunity was taken to reorganise and train the levies. A third shipment of reinforcements from England brought out the 3rd Hussars KGL, two batteries of the KGA, the British 73rd Regiment, and a rocket detachment of the Royal Artillery.

When hostilities recommenced the French moved against the left wing of the northern allies to begin a series of manoeuvres and actions that culminated in the battle of the Göhrde on 18 September 1813 when, with a force of 5,000 infantry, 2,800 cavalry and 28 guns, Wallmoden attacked the French force of Gen Pecheux, which initially fell back in good order. At this point the KGL 3rd Hussars charged the French infantry, breaking into their squares and starting a rout in which the enemy lost nearly 2,000 killed and wounded and 1,500 prisoners (included a general seized by a KGL hussar, and two colonels). Among the Allied losses of 550 were 95 officers and men of the 3rd Hussars.

Operations in northern Germany continued until October, when the Allied victory at Leipzig gave fresh impetus to the advance to the Rhine. (Present at the battle of Leipzig was Lt Charles Poten of the KGL's 7th Line Battalion. Poten had been with Halkett's party, but had conducted a British rocket battery to the grand army in Saxony.) Wallmoden's force now took Hanover and reinforced Lüneburg as the Allies moved to the Weser, blockading Davout and his forces in Hamburg, and forcing their

Danish collaborators to retire northwards into Holstein. There, in December, Wallmoden's forces were driven back after a costly battle with the Danes at Sehestadt. A peace was then concluded, after which the 3rd Hussars and the KGL horse artillery were ordered to proceed to Holland and to join the forces under Gen Sir Thomas Graham, Wellington's former second-in-command. The plan was for an Anglo-Prussian force to capture the port of Antwerp. However, the Prussians failed to carry out their part in the scheme, and after the British force had managed to capture Bergen-op-Zoom, 25 miles north of the port, they were driven off and failed in their aim.

1813: VICTORY IN SPAIN

In the Peninsula, the winter of 1812/13 was spent by Wellington reorganising his forces for the coming campaigning season. The outbreak of war with the United States had limited his reinforcements, the losses of the 1812 campaign needed to be made up, and the sick returned to duty; but by the spring of 1813 Wellington had available 100,000 men – British, Portuguese and Spanish. This was a small enough force for the task ahead, but the French were also experiencing manpower problems. Their terrible losses in Russia and the consequently hurried raising of new armies did not merely cut short the supply of reinforcements to Spain. Desperate for experienced men, Napoleon recalled Marshal Soult, the Imperial Guard units posted there, and quotas of veterans from the line regiments in Spain to put backbone into his newly-conscripted units; 15,000 Frenchmen marched northwards out of Spain. King Joseph and Marshal Jourdan pulled back their remaining forces, abandoning the south and the north-west of Spain. In March 1813 Madrid was abandoned by the French as they withdrew ever closer to the Pyrenees and the border with France to await the onslaught of Wellington and his forces.

The deployment of the King's German Legion had undergone various changes over the course of the winter. The 2nd Hussars, who had experienced hard campaigning and suffered severe losses, were ordered to hand over their horses to other cavalry units and to embark for England for reinforcement and remounts. The Light battalions of the Legion joined the three Line battalions in the 1st Division to make a five-battalion KGL Brigade under Col Halkett. (The other brigade in the division was the Guards Brigade, which included the 1st Battalion of the Coldstream Guards and the 1st/3rd Guards.)

In March an Anglo-Sicilian force, which had been co-operating with Spanish troops in eastern Spain since the previous August, moved against the French forces in Valencia. The Allied force mustered 30,000 men under LtGen Sir John Murray, and included the 4th and 6th Line Battalions KGL, the skirmishers of the 3rd and 8th Line Battalions, and artillery from the KGA 3rd Foot Battery. The French forces amounted to

Castell's drawing of an officer of the 2nd Light Bn shows a rifle-green jacket of a cut very different from those of the officers of the 1st Light. No marks of rank seem to have been worn on the shoulders; three rows of buttons and black cording decorated its front; and there were no skirts. Note the 'mirleton' cap, depicted here with gold cords; the 1803 pattern light company sabre, and the black leather pouch and sword belts. The trousers are shown as dark grey. (Author's collection)

18,000 men holding positions along the Xucar river south of Valencia. On 6 March the Allies drove the French from their advanced positions and eventually halted in front of the walled town of Villena, which was then garrisoned by a regiment of Spanish troops. Here Murray sat until 11 April, when he became aware that the French had assembled a strong force of cavalry to the north of the town. Later in the day, when the French cavalry began to advance, Murray retired with his main force, leaving the garrison of Villena to its fate, and a force of infantry to defend the Biar pass through which he had withdrawn.

The defending force consisted of the British 2nd/27th (Enniskillen) Regiment, the skirmishers of the Legion's 3rd and 8th Line Battalions, the Italians of the Calabrian Free Corps, the 1st Italian Regiment, a troop of the Foreign Hussars and four mountain guns. Commanded by a Col Adams, who had orders to fall back on the Allies' main position at Castalla if attacked, this forerunner of the international brigades of the 1930s was indeed attacked by the French, 5,000 of them, at noon on the 12th. Taking up fire positions on the heights of the pass, Adams' light troops kept the enemy at bay for five hours while the rest of his command fell back in good order on Castalla. There, on the following day, a battle was fought in which all units of the KGL distinguished themselves. Although the French were beaten, however, the irresolute British commander allowed the enemy to leave the field without a proper pursuit.

In his report Murray claimed the French losses to be 3,000 men, but the French admitted to losing only 800. Allied losses were over 600, not including the 1,000-strong garrison of Villena which chose to surrender rather than face impossible odds. Legion losses were 58 men. (During the battle 12 skirmishers of the 4th Line Battalion became isolated and were forced to take cover in a wine press, surrounded by the enemy. Here they fought off their attackers, refusing all offers of surrender, and were eventually relieved by the Enniskillens.)

As the enemy drew off Murray marched his men back to Alicante to embark. He then sailed to Tarragona, which he besieged for only eight days before hastening away on learning that superior French forces were marching to raise the siege. In his haste to reach the safety of his ships Murray left behind 19 pieces of artillery, for which he was subsequently court-martialled. He was replaced by Lord William Bentinck.

In May 1813 Wellington set his army in motion, crossing into Spain and advancing on Salamanca with half of his force, while Sir Thomas Graham with the remainder – which included the two Dragoon regiments of the Legion and the five

A private soldier of the 2nd Light Bn, c.1815. Castell shows his rifle-green jacket with the same three rows of buttons as his officer, black-tufted shoulder straps, and small skirts behind. His shako has a ball tuft, bugle-horn badge and black cords. Equipment is of black leather and he carries a Baker rifle. (Author's collection)

KGL battalions in the 1st Division – moved rapidly northwards to outflank a series of potential defensive lines on the French right. As if mesmerised, the enemy fell back before Wellington, apparently unaware that 40,000 men were about to hit them in the flank. Contact was made on the 31st at Morales in a cavalry clash that left a French regiment cut to pieces, and revealed to King Joseph the danger that now faced him. He ordered a retreat, pursued by the forces of Wellington, now re-united under their commander. Burgos was abandoned by the French after they had blown up its fortress on the night of 12/13 June. Reaching the Ebro river, Joseph and Jourdan deployed their forces for battle; but Wellington outflanked them by crossing the river further north to force the French to pull back to Vittoria where, on 19 June, they once more deployed their army to fight.

The Iberian Peninsula, showing the locations of some of the KGL's actions 1812-1814.

The battle of Vittoria

The battle was fought on 21 June, its outcome being a resounding victory for Wellington, a crushing defeat for the French, and an end to their control of Spain. Few of the KGL units were actively involved, but

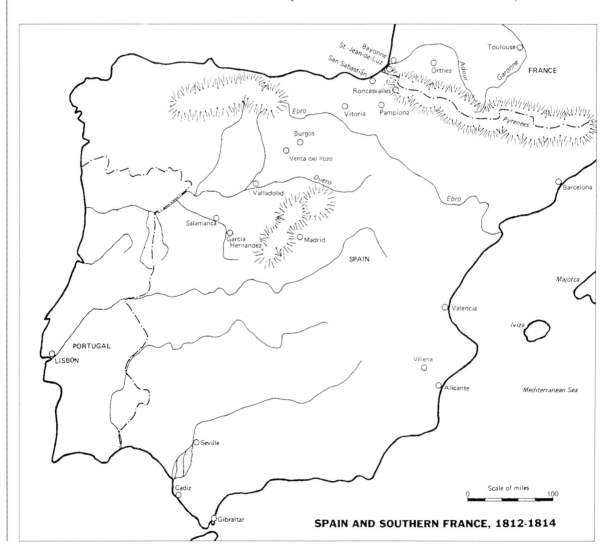

SPAIN AND SOUTHERN FRANCE, 1812-1814

the Light battalions took part in the capture of the village of Abechuco which blocked the enemy's line of retreat to Bayonne. The subsequent flight of the French left their artillery and baggage train in the hands of the victorious Allied soldiers, who found themselves in possession of millions in gold coin, an accumulation of loot that the French had plundered from Portugal and Spain, and the baggage of the household of King Joseph. Discipline vanished in a frenzy of looting as soldiers fought each other in their greed while their officers looked on, not daring to interfere. Of the 5½ million dollars known to have been in the French camp, only 100,000 reached Wellington's military chest. Commissary Schaumann of the KGL, an eyewitness to the aftermath of the battle, described the devastation of the scene after the plunderers had moved on, commenting that many men – particularly those who found diamonds – became rich that day. It has since been claimed that never before or since has such a quantity of treasure been taken on a battlefield.

Wellington fumed that the night of the battle was spent by his men in looking for loot – and cheerfully auctioning it around their campfires – instead of resting, the consequence being that they were 'totally knocked up' and unable to march in pursuit of the enemy next morning. They were 'the scum of the earth', 'vagabond soldiers'; it was impossible to keep 'such men as some of our soldiers are' in order. He did not spare some of their officers, either; after the retreat from Burgos he had written that 'Nobody in the British army ever reads a regulation or an order...in any other manner than as an amusing novel'. (They nevertheless won him promotion to field-marshal for the triumph at Vittoria.)

The siege of San Sebastian

Eventually discipline was restored and the army followed the French, who occupied the fortresses of Pamplona and San Sebastian while fighting a series of rearguard actions as they withdrew into France. One such was at Tolosa, where the units of the KGL Brigade suffered 170 casualties in clearing the enemy from the town. At San Sebastian the French garrison, secure behind the stout walls of their town and citadel and supplied nightly by small craft from Bayonne, were determined to deny the harbour to the Allies for as long as possible. Pamplona was invested by Spanish troops on 26 June, and Gen Graham's corps, which included the 1st Division with the KGL Brigade, had laid siege to San Sebastian by early July.

Wellington needed this harbour, close to the French frontier, for the support of his current and future operations. With his siege forces were LtCol Hartmann of the King's German Artillery, commanding the

A Castell line-and-wash depiction of a grenadier company soldier of a KGL Line battalion, c.1815. Here the artist has been less than accurate, failing to show the lace on the breast of the jacket as five pairs, showing the tufting of the wings but not the wings themselves, and drawing his musket very badly. However, the basic details are correct, including the dark blue line in the jacket lace. (Author's collection)

breaching artillery of the left wing; and the infantry of the KGL, who were employed initially on covering duties but from 17 July assisted in the trenches around the fortress. Breaching commenced and the first attempt at an assault was made on the 25th by infantry of the 5th Division. This was bloodily repulsed with great loss of life. A decision was taken to await the arrival of more powerful guns from England, and to make the next assault with a body of volunteers. In the meantime the blockade of the garrison was continued. By 24 August the ordnance had arrived and bombardment recommenced. By the 30th the breaches made were considered to be practicable, and on the following day the final assault was made by a brigade of the 5th Division supported by 750 volunteers, including 200 men of the King's German Legion.

At 11 o'clock on 31 August the assault was launched in a hail of fire and exploding mines that all but annihilated the leading stormers. For two hours a way into the defences was sought, at great cost, until a decision was taken to concentrate the fire of 47 guns on one of the breaches while the attackers picked their way through this early example of overhead fire. To the artillery was added the fire of the riflemen in the trenches before the breach. As the barrage began it ignited the explosives and combustibles which the defenders had prepared to hurl down on the attackers, and into this inferno dashed the British and German stormers. After capturing the defences above the breach they drove the French back into the citadel, which was bombarded for a further eight days until, on 9 September, the remainder of the garrison surrendered with the honours of war.

The price for the capture of San Sebastian was 3,780 Allied casualties, the final assault alone costing 500 dead and 1,500 wounded. Legion losses were 19 killed and 48 wounded. Yet again the victory was tarnished by the subsequent behaviour of the surviving stormers, which it was said 'would have shamed the most ferocious barbarians of antiquity'. After any bloody assault the battle-crazed survivors indulged in drunkenness, rape, murder and looting; but at San Sebastian atrocities of 'indescribable barbarity' were perpetrated on the civil population. Commissary Schaumann, visiting the scene afterwards, describes the town as devastated, its buildings burned and in ruins, the streets full of debris, and with decomposing corpses everywhere.

An army of 80,000 men under Marshal Soult had been put together from the remnants of the French forces which had escaped into France after Vittoria. In July he had attempted to raise the siege of Pamplona, but had been checked and then driven off at Sorauren. He tried to

Castell drawing of an officer of 'skirmishers' of a KGL Line battalion, c.1815. His shako has a green plume and gold-and-red cords; his scarlet jacket has gold lace, fringed gold wings, and dark blue facings. His sash is of the light infantry pattern, his overalls are light grey, and the belt supporting his 1803 pattern sabre is of black leather. (Author's collection)

relieve San Sebastian in late August but was again driven off. Pamplona was starved into submission and capitulated on 31 October.

On the Catalonian coast Lord William Bentinck's mixed force continued to harass the French by raiding from the sea. September found them confronting a much stronger French force before Barcelona. An advanced group of about 1,000 men – including British from the 27th (Enniskillen) Regiment, Germans from the 4th Line Battalion KGL, and Swiss from the Regiment de Roll – were attacked by a strong force of French while holding a redoubt on the Villafranca road. Bentinck's men held their position for a considerable time, were driven out of it, retook it with the help of Spanish troops, were driven out again, and once again retook it. Only when outflanked were they obliged finally to give it up and retire to their waiting ships. The KGL element suffered 36 casualties in this bravely fought action.

RIGHT **Horse artilleryman of the KGA, c.1815. Castell shows a Tarleton helmet and a dark blue jacket with red facings and yellow cording. He is armed with a 1796 pattern light cavalry sabre carried on a shoulder belt and slings. On active service grey overalls would have been worn instead of the white breeches shown here. (Author's collection)**

FAR RIGHT **Castell's depiction of a private soldier of foot artillery, KGA, c.1815. He wears a white tuft and yellow cords on his shako; his dark blue jacket is faced red and laced yellow. His artillery hanger is carried on a shoulder belt of whitened buff leather, and his overalls are grey. His shako plate seems to differ from the British regulation item of the time, but one source gives that for the KGA as the arms of the Board of Ordnance – three cannons on a shield – and Castell may have attempted to show such a badge here. (Author's collection)**

Into France

With San Sebastian available to him as a supply port Wellington was in a position to enter France, which he did by crossing the river Bidassoa on 7 October 1813. On the coast his troops took Hendaye. Further inland the 1st Division, led by the Light battalions of the KGL, waded the river to force the French from their prepared defence positions. One KGL participant describes his unit being up to their armpits in water, knee deep in mud, and holding their weapons above the water while the enemy's musket balls splashed 'around us like a shower of rain'- and all this, he complained, without the benefit of breakfast. Further inland still, the Light Division and a division of Spanish troops battled to seize the Bera pass and the La Rhune massif against stiff opposition, the latter not falling until the following day. For the cost of 1,560 casualties – 123 of them among the KGL units – Wellington had a toehold in France.

He now paused to wait for the fall of Pamplona and to consider the courses of action open to him. Fearing that his Spanish troops, with so much to avenge, would commit excesses amongst the French civil population, he sent all but the most trusted of them back to Spanish territory. Reconnaissance showed him that the French defences along the river Nivelle were strongest on their right or coastal flank where Marshal Soult expected his main attack, as at the Bidassoa. The French line of entrenchments and redoubts continued to be improved as Wellington waited; but when Pamplona's capitulation on 31 October freed the forces under Sir Rowland Hill to march to join him, he was ready to attack.

The Nivelle

At 3 o'clock on the morning of 10 November 1813 Wellington's troops silently descended upon the advanced picquets of the French defences. Choosing not to concentrate on Soult's strongly defended right wing, Wellington directed his main efforts on the enemy's centre and left. However, the 1st and 5th Divisions (now commanded by LtGen Sir John Hope, Sir Thomas Graham having given up command in order to lead an expedition to Holland) were ordered to feint against Soult's main position. This operation was described by Ensign Edmund Wheatley, a junior officer with the 5th Line Battalion, as beginning in the early hours as they crept up to the French lines to surprise and capture their outposts before closing silently on their main position; they then lay down, waiting for daybreak. When dawn came the French poured fire from their batteries upon them as they supported an attempt to take the fortified village of Urrugne. Wheatley and his men took up a position in a house from which they shot at the French before being driven off by a counter-attack. His anxieties were allayed when he observed his commanding officer, LtCol Christian von Ompteda, joking with his young nephews as the French cannon shot tore the earth and roared by. (These boys, the eldest an ensign in the 6th Line Battalion, were only 16 and 14 years old.) Wheatley was wounded the next day, taking no further part in the feint; but the operation had the effect of causing the enemy to abandon his position with the loss of 50 pieces of artillery.

Wellington's attacks on the weaker centre and left of the French line had been carried out with great success, breaking through the enemy line, outflanking the entire defence system, and forcing the French to

A Castell line-and-wash drawing of an officer of Engineers, KGL, c.1815. A small officer-only unit, the engineers wore scarlet jackets faced black. Castell's subject is shown wearing a cocked hat with a red-over-white falling feather plume and gold loop, button and tasselled pulls; a single gold epaulette; a black leather sword belt, and grey overalls. He is armed with some pattern of sabre. (Author's collection)

A water-colour sketch of a
private of the 2nd Light
Dragoons, KGL, 1814. The
German artist has made a
number of errors of detail
(including a third suspension
strap for the sabretasche and
a marked lack of curvature to
the sabre), but has captured
the essence of the German
cavalryman, with his pipe and
moustaches. The English infantry
officer Edmund Wheatley
described his men when off-duty
as either smoking, cooking,
eating or drinking; the
same must have applied
to the cavalry of the
KGL. Pipes were either
the elaborate German
types or the simpler
English clay pipes –
as here. (Bomann
Museum, Celle)

fall back on Bayonne. Soult lost more than 4,000 men in the day's fighting, Allied losses being 2,600, of which 159 were from the units of the King's German Legion. In the days that followed the weather broke, with icy rain lashing the troops of both sides and turning roads and encampments into morasses.

1814: SOUTHERN FRANCE

In the aftermath of the battle for the Nivelle both commanders faced difficult decisions. The hardly surprising behaviour of the Spanish troops after the battle, when they indulged themselves in looting, rape and arson, forced Wellington to order them to return to Spain: he could not afford to risk having the French civil population rise up against him as had the Spanish against their invaders. The departure of all but 4,500 of the Spanish reduced the Allied army to 63,000 men, inferior in numbers to that of the French – but a veteran army, much superior to their conscripts.

Soult came to the conclusion that strongly fortified defence lines were of little use against Wellington, who seemed to be able to break through them or march around them at will. He therefore devised a form of defence in depth, concentrating his forces behind a screen of strong patrols whose task it was to guard the bridges and fords and to give notice of Allied movement.

On 9 December 1813 they had much to report, as Wellington's troops crossed the river Nive. Soult counter-attacked on the 10th and again on the 13th, striking first at Wellington's right and then at his left, both attacks being repulsed at a cost to the French of 6,000 casualties. (Part of these losses were the regiments of Frankfurt and Nassau-Usingen which, under the command of a Col Kruse, defected to the Allies on the 10th.) Allied losses in these battles were reckoned at 5,029 men, the KGL units suffering 70 of this total.

These harassing battles were the last stirrings of both armies in the 1813 campaigning season before going into encampment to endure the bitter winter weather, after which a kind of peace reigned until the February of 1814.

It was at this time that the order was received converting the two Dragoon regiments of the KGL into regiments of Light Dragoons. At this time also Napoleon was scraping together yet another army after his defeat at Leipzig. From Soult's army he withdrew two infantry divisions, a cavalry division and five batteries of artillery, leaving him only 40,000 men to confront Wellington.

As the news reached southern France of the Austrian, Prussian and Russian invasion in the north, Wellington's British, KGL and Portuguese troops made ready to resume the offensive (they were later rejoined by some Spanish formations). The Allied forces were divided into three columns; the 1st Division – which included the five infantry battalions of the KGL – marched in the left wing column under Sir John Hope. The

Light Dragoons and the 1st Hussars of the Legion were with the Cavalry Division, while Maj Sympher's battery of the KGA marched with the 4th Division.

On 13 February Wellington moved on Bordeaux, sending a column under Gen Hill to attempt to turn Soult's positions along the river Ardour. Hope's wing was sent to lay siege to Bayonne, held by a single French division. Soult attempted to halt Wellington at Orthez on 27 February, but was beaten in a battle which numbered Maj Sympher of the KGA among the casualties; bravely handling his battery under heavy counter-fire, Sympher was struck in the chest by a cannon shot and killed instantly.

On the same day the infantry of the KGL were engaged in heavy fighting before Bayonne, which

German water-colour sketch of a grenadier company private of a Line battalion of the KGL, c.1815. The artist was probably more familiar with French weapons than British: he has drawn his subject's musket with barrel bands. Other than that, the uniform details are fairly accurate, down to the 'worm' lace of the coat. However, the subject is shown with dark blue wings and turnbacks – an error perpetrated by Charles Hamilton Smith (see MAA 338, page 20) and frequently copied ever since. Therefore, even though the caption to the sketch shows it to be German, the source is obvious. (Bomann Museum, Celle)

RIGHT German water-colour sketch of an officer of a KGL Line battalion, c.1815. As in the previous illustration the artist has perpetuated at least one of Hamilton Smith's errors – dark blue turnbacks – which are also shown on what is either an oddly long-tailed jacket or a short-tailed coat! Tailors' instructions of the time called for 'A jacket made of super fine cloth, dark blue lapels, cuffs and collars – white casimere turnbacks, ditto skirt linings – no lace for the turnbacks' for officers of KGL Line units. The sword shown is the 1796 pattern for infantry officers. A straight-bladed parry-and-thrust weapon, it was undoubtedly more suited to the confines of close formations than the sabres of flank company officers. (Bomann Museum, Celle)

Dragoner
vom 1. und vom 2. leichten Dragoner-Regiment.

Offiziere
vom 1. und vom 2. leichten Dragoner-Regiment.

Englisch-Deutsche Legion.
1814.

Plate by Richard Knötel depicting officers and men of the Light Dragoons of the KGL in 1814. By this time the transition from 'heavy' dragoons had been completed, at least as far as uniforms and weapons were concerned. Saddlery and harness had an extraordinarily long life, and the heavy cavalry patterns of saddles, etc, were probably retained. Equally, it is doubtful that the larger horses of the 1st and 2nd Dragoons would have been exchanged for the lighter horses ridden by hussars and light dragoon regiments. Perhaps the giving up of the heavy swords they had wielded to such effect at Garcia Hernandez and other actions, in return for the lighter curved sabre of the hussars, caused the newly 'lightened' dragoons some regret? (Author's collection)

had been encircled by the Allies the day before. Given the task of capturing the northern suburb of St Etienne, the men of the Line battalions were subjected to intense fire from the batteries covering the fortified village, but pushed forward to within 200 yards of the citadel's defences, capturing a gun as they went. Sheltering in the village church after its capture, a young officer of the 5th Line recorded how the noise of the French batteries and the falling glass brought down by musketry quite bewildered him in such a peaceful setting. He had little time to muse on the contradiction before Col von Ompteda ordered those in the church to follow him, leading three companies of his battalion into further hard fighting at the French entrenchments on the Bayonne high road.

Ordered to defend a building, the young officer entered it with 15 men only to endure a blistering fire as the house was broken up about them by the fire of French heavy cannon. His men were reduced to six when the bombardment brought down the roof, burying them all. He clambered from the wreckage, covered in plaster and 'as white as a miller', and was joined by his sergeant and three men – the sole survivors. The casualties for the 5th Line Battalion that day numbered 113 officers and men. Reckoned against the total of 371 casualties suffered by all the KGL units on 27 February, they show that the 5th had the misfortune to be in the thick of the battle and receiving a disproportionate amount of French fire.

The citadel of Bayonne remained under siege for the next two months, with infantry units of the

17

KGL sharing duty in the trenches, standing guard or digging, always under the fire of the French garrison. When news reached Bayonne on 10 April that the Allies had occupied Paris and that Napoleon had been deposed the garrison commander determined on one last gesture of defiance, sending his men out on a sortie against the besiegers on the night of the 14th. This attack captured St Etienne and threw the Allied forces into disarray. The KGL units had been out of the line, but rapidly stood to arms and once again drove the French from St Etienne after daybreak. This wholly unnecessary battle cost the Allies 800 casualties (including Gen Sir John Hope and his staff made prisoners), of which nearly 200 were from the Legion. Bayonne finally capitulated on 28 April.

While the left wing of his army had been engaged at Bayonne Wellington had been following up his victory at Orthez, with the KGL Light Dragoons distinguishing themselves on 19 March when they drove in the enemy rearguard at Vic Bigorre. As the Allied centre and right wings pushed forward, Soult and his army fell back to expose Bordeaux (which was first entered by a squadron of the 1st Hussars KGL on 12 March), and then to take up positions at Toulouse. There, on 10 April 1814, a final battle was fought in which the cavalry and artillery of the Legion distinguished themselves. This action ended with the defeat of the French, but might never have been fought had the news of Napoleon's abdication arrived earlier than 12 April.

Elsewhere units of the KGL saw action when an Allied force under Lord William Bentinck landed at Leghorn in northern Italy on 9 March 1814. Among his troops were the 3rd, 6th and 8th Line Battalions and detachments of the King's German Artillery. On the 27th Spezia was entered, and on 17 April Genoa was attacked, capitulating the following day.

By now news of the events in Paris was widespread, and all combatant forces were aware that a peace treaty had been signed and that Napoleon was on his way to exile on Elba. It seemed to all Europe that after a quarter of a century of turmoil peace had at last prevailed.

1815: THE WATERLOO CAMPAIGN

Scarcely had the Treaty of Fontainbleau brought an end to hostilities than Wellington's army of veterans began to be broken up. Wellington himself left for London to receive the rewards of a grateful nation, honours and wealth. His soldiers were less fortunate. Some were sent to the continuing war with the United States, others went home for discharge. In August Wellington, by now elevated to the rank of duke and £500,000 richer, travelled to Paris to become British ambassador to the court of the restored King Louis XVIII.

Arthur Wellesley, 1st Duke of Wellington (1769-1852), by Sir Thomas Lawrence. The unpromising fifth son of an Irish peer, he purchased into the 73rd Highlanders in 1787, then served in several other regiments, becoming captain in 1791 and lieutenant-colonel in 1793. He went to India with the 33rd Foot in 1796, and led a brigade against Tipoo Sahib, after which he became governor of Seringapatam and commander of the forces in Mysore. After several victories over the Mahrattas he returned to England, was knighted, and entered Parliament in 1807. He took part in the expedition to Denmark in that year, operating with units of the KGL for the first time (see MAA 338). After a string of victories over the French in the Peninsula, and the defeat of Napoleon at Waterloo,

(continued opposite)

As for the King's German Legion, a decision was made to keep these valuable troops for the time being, and they were gradually moved from southern France to Flanders, the cavalry and artillery overland and the infantry by sea. By early 1815 the KGL units concentrated there comprised:

1st Light Dragoons	(in Gen von Dornberg's brigade)
2nd Light Dragoons	
1st Hussars	(in Gen Vivian's brigade)
2nd Hussars	(in Gen Grant's brigade)
3rd Hussars	(in Col von Arentschild's brigade)
1st Light Battalion	
2nd Light Battalion	(Col von Ompteda's 2nd KGL brigade,
5th Line Battalion	3rd Division)
8th Line Battalion	
1st Line Battalion	
2nd Line Battalion	(Col du Plat's 1st KGL brigade,
3rd Line Battalion	2nd Division)
4th Line Battalion	
1st Foreign Veteran Bn	(Antwerp garrison)
1st Horse Battery	(2nd Division)
2nd Horse Battery	(1st Division)
4th Foot Battery	(3rd Division)
1st Artillery Company	(Operating as fortress artillery
2nd Artillery Company	and reinforcements.)

By this time nearly all non-Hanoverian rank-and-file – the thousands of men from other German states, Austria, Prussia, Holland, Belgium, Poland and Switzerland who had given valuable service in the ranks of the Legion – had been discharged or transferred to other foreign corps. There was great competition for recruits between the Legion and the expanding Hanoverian Army. Within battalions the number of companies was reduced from ten to six, and troops in cavalry regiments from eight to six; surplus officers and non-commissioned officers were posted to Hanoverian Landwehr battalions. Thus, although greatly reduced in numbers for the battles to come (about 7,000 at Waterloo), the KGL was once again a truly Hanoverian formation, its mix of veterans and young soldiers benefiting once more from the national cohesion of the Legion's earliest days.

In January 1815 the Duke of Wellington travelled to Vienna to take part in the Congress of powers deciding how Europe was to be divided and ruled in the future. There, on 7 March 1815, news was received that the deposed Emperor of the French had evaded his British naval watchdogs, had left Elba with the 1,000 soldiers of his retinue, and was at large. Wellington guessed correctly that Bonaparte would head for Paris. Landing near Cannes, Napoleon marched north, his small force growing as he commandeered horses and supplies, and as regiment after regiment hastened to join his colours.

the Duke of Wellington (as he had by then become) was appointed commander of the Allied occupation of Paris until 1818. He then returned to a life of politics, becoming Prime Minister in 1828-30. He retired from public office in 1846 and was appointed Lord High Constable of England in 1848. He died at Walmer Castle, Kent, four years later and was buried in St Paul's Cathedral, the most famous and revered man of his age.

His brilliance as a general brought him honours, riches and fame; he owed no small part of them to the tough and hard-fighting men of the armies he led – particularly in the Peninsula. Wellington was always sparing with his praise, but he held the KGL in high regard, especially their cavalry. (Author's collection)

On 19 March Louis XVIII fled from Paris, and the following day Napoleon entered the city in triumph. By early April he was once again organising an army to lead against the forces which the Allies were assembling to maintain the Treaty of Paris. By late May half a million men of the Allied armies were committed to converge on the borders of France, but a high proportion of these were still far away and moving slowly. With his own more limited resources Napoleon determined to destroy them in detail before they had a chance to mass – a strategy he had employed with dazzling successs in the past. At the head of the 123,000 men and 366 guns of his Army of the North he set out to destroy the Anglo-Dutch and Prussian armies in Belgium, and had concentrated his force on the Franco-Belgian frontier by 14 June 1815.

Across that border the Allied forces were encamped awaiting orders to advance into France. In and around Brussels was the field force of the Army of the Netherlands, commanded by the Duke of Wellington and consisting of 107,000 men and 196 guns. Commanding the Prussian army in the Liege area was Field-Marshal von Blücher with 128,000 men and 312 guns. While the Prussian and French armies were national forces each with a common language, common traditions and common loyalties, the Army of the Netherlands was not; and it was this polyglot quality which led Wellington to call it an 'infamous army'. Only ten of its infantry brigades were British. Eleven brigades were composed of KGL or Hanoverian Army units; seven were Dutch or Belgian; two were from Brunswick, and one from Nassau – ten British brigades to twenty-one others.

More than a few of the non-British troops had, at one time or another, carried muskets or sabres for Napoleon, including significant numbers of officers of the Dutch-Belgian forces (and the Nassauers of Gen von Kruse, last encountered by the KGL in southern France). In the cavalry the proportion of British was slightly greater, but overall Wellington's command was as much German as it was Anglo-Dutch – a raw and untried army with few veteran units. The few British units which had served in the Peninsula by now contained many recent recruits and transferred militiamen; the latter were well trained and disciplined, but few had yet smelt powder. Apart from these battalions only the KGL, down in numbers though they were, still contained a high proportion of officers and men with experience of battle.

Quatre-Bras

On 15 June Napoleon's forces crossed the Belgian frontier at Charleroi divided into two wings and a reserve. Catching the Allies off balance, the emperor sent his left wing under Ney

The farm of La Haye Sainte today, looking roughly east to west; the modern highway follows the line of the old Brussels-Charleroi road. The buildings have changed little since their defence by the KGL on 18 June 1815. Gone are the orchards to the south (left) of the buildings, and the embankment to the north of the main building has been levelled. Otherwise the layout and structure of the farm still closely resemble the maps and paintings made at the time of the battle.

Fighting raged and swirled around the bastion of La Haye Sainte for most of the day, until its garrison was forced to evacuate it through lack of ammunition. Colonel von Ompteda was killed while leading an attack on French troops who had occupied the garden which was north (right) of the house in the area now bordered by the road, the prominent hedgerow and the tall tree. (Author's collection)

to advance to contact against Wellington, and his right against Blücher. On the 16th Napoleon's left wing fought a bruising battle with Anglo-Dutch troops at the vital crossroads of Quatre-Bras, held at first only by a well-led Dutch-Belgian brigade but progressively reinforced during the day by Allied units arriving to join in a scrambling but ultimately successful defence. Further east the French right wing encountered the Prussians, who had taken up positions around Ligny on the north bank of the river Ligne. Against them Napoleon threw his major effort; the battle developed into a killing match, and the roughly-handled Prussians withdrew at nightfall towards Wavre. Their losses at Ligny were 16,000 against 12,000 French casualties, but Napoleon had not destroyed them as he had intended. Blücher's army had undergone a mauling, but it was still in being, and falling back in good order under the command of the injured but indomitable old marshal and his brilliant chief-of-staff Gen von Gneisenau.

At nightfall on the 16th Quatre-Bras was still held by Wellington, but on hearing of the Prussian withdrawal he decided to conform with his ally. By mid-morning on 17 June he had issued orders to his army to fall back on Waterloo, long ago selected as a possible battlefield. Napoleon displayed an extraordinary lassitude, and an imprecision in his orders to his senior subordinates. As a result Wellington was able to withdraw without serious interference, and Grouchy's corps, following the Prussians from Ligny, did not prevent Blücher from converging on Wellington's next planned position.

So far the King's German Legion had been little involved. Major Kuhlmann's horse artillery battery and Capt Cleeve's foot artillery battery had both come into action at Quatre-Bras on the afternoon of the 16th, and Col von Ompteda's brigade had arrived that night after the fighting had died down. During the withdrawal from Quatre-Bras both regiments of KGL Light Dragoons performed rearguard duties, masking the retirement of the marching troops and harassing the French cavalry advance guards. (A troop of the 2nd Light Dragoons took part with the British 7th Hussars in one such action, in which they were able to recover three wagons full of captured British wounded.)

Waterloo

Under torrential rain – which continued from the afternoon of the 17th to the early morning of the 18th – Wellington deployed the Army of the Netherlands on an east-west rise astride the main Charleroi-Brussels road, just south of the Forest of Soignes near a hamlet called Mont St Jean. The position was a few miles from the village of Waterloo, where he set up his headquarters. It was strongly suited for defence, the slight ridge being sufficient to command the low ground south of it each side of the main road up which the French were following. Wellington's line – anchored on the flanks and in the centre by farms and villages which were turned into small fortresses – was almost completely hidden from view.

The events that took place around Mont St Jean on Sunday 18 June 1815 are too well known to repeat here in great detail. Sufficient to say that Napoleon displayed once more an uncharacteristic lack of energy and grip. Not expecting Wellington to stand for any longer than was necessary to allow his wagons to continue their withdrawal through the

Charles, Count Alten (1764-1840), colonel-commandant of the 1st Light Bn and major-general commanding the 3rd Division at Waterloo, where he was severely wounded. He later become a general in the Hanoverian Army, Inspector-General of Hanoverian Forces and Minister at War.

It was Alten who, on the evacuation of La Haye Sainte, ordered Col von Ompteda to advance his 5th Line Battalion KGL *in line* to attack the French infantry pursuing the garrison. Von Ompteda protested, saying that he had seen French cavalry through the smoke. The Prince of Orange, observing the argument, then ordered Von Ompteda to obey Alten's order – and was rewarded with the blame for the disaster that then befell the 5th Line. (Author's drawing after Heaphy)

forest just north of the position, and frustrated in his desire to attack at once by the boggy condition of the fields, from about 11.30am until 7.30pm he threw wave after wave of infantry and cavalry northwards against the Anglo-Dutch position until his troops were exhausted. At this point pressure from Blücher's Prussians, coming up fast from the east, created a retreat that became a rout, and Napoleon's last battle was lost.

The deployment of the units of the Legion at the start of the battle was thus (see map below):

Colonel von Ompteda's 2nd KGL Brigade held ground in the centre of Wellington's position, with the 2nd Light Battalion defending the farm of La Haye Sainte and the remaining three battalions in rear. Colonel du Plat's 1st KGL Brigade was positioned several hundred yards to the rear of the manor of Hougoumont, on Wellington's right. On the extreme left flank were the 1st Hussars. The 1st and 2nd Light Dragoons were positioned to the left of Du Plat's infantry, and behind them were the 3rd Hussars. (The 2nd Hussars were absent, on outpost duties on the French frontier in Flanders.) The artillery of the Legion all had their guns positioned between La Haye Sainte and Hougoumont, the two fortified positions before the Anglo-Dutch line which the French had to take before assaulting the main position. (Hougoumont was garrisoned by four light companies of British Foot Guards, the 1/2nd Nassau Light Infantry and a company of Hanoverian riflemen.)

By about 11.30am the rain-soaked ground was considered dry enough to be passable, and the battle began with an attack upon Hougoumont.

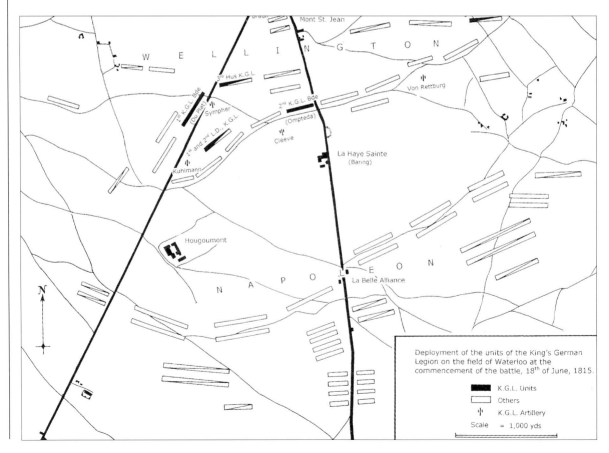

Deployment of the units of the King's German Legion on the field of Waterloo at the commencement of the battle, 18th of June, 1815.

K.G.L. Units

Others

K.G.L. Artillery

Scale = 1,000 yds

This was halted and beaten off with the aid of fire from Capt Cleeve's battery. The manor was to be fought over throughout the battle, but remained in Allied hands while more and more units were drawn into its defence, including the KGL 2nd Line Battalion. Serving with this battalion was the redoubtable Christian Hallego, who had exhibited such remarkable bravery at the siege of Burgos. At Hougoumont he led the recapture of the gardens, making two Frenchmen prisoner and clearing the way with blows from the butt of his musket. Another KGL hero at Hougoumont was Cpl Christian Brinkmann of the 3rd Line, who captured a French staff officer there by leaping a hedge, seizing his horse's bridle, and dragging him off within sight of his own men.

Baring at La Haye Sainte

As the French attacks on Hougoumont began the defenders of the farm of La Haye Sainte stood to their arms. The garrison consisted of six companies of the KGL 2nd Light Battalion under the command of Maj George Baring – less than 400 men. Baring positioned three companies in the orchard nearest the enemy, two in the farm buildings, and one in the gardens to the rear. A barricade had been built across the main road beside the position, but little could be done to improve the defences of the farm, as all the battalion's pioneers and tools had been sent to help fortify Hougoumont the night before. Nevertheless, the men of the 2nd Light did what they could with their bayonets and bare hands to cut loopholes and throw up breastworks. Major Baring's account takes up the story (we have modernised some of his punctuation for greater clarity):

'Shortly after noon some skirmishers commenced the attack ... The enemy did not spend long skirmishing, but immediately advanced over the height [presumably the elevated ground at La Belle Alliance south of the farm] in two close columns, one of which attacked the buildings while the other threw itself *en masse* into the orchard, showing the greatest contempt for our fire. It was not possible for our small, dispersed force fully to withstand this furious attack by such a superior force, and we retired

23

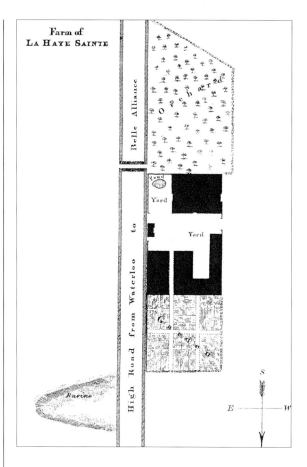

Farm of
LA HAYE SAINTE

Belle Alliance

to

Orchard

Yard

Yard

High Road from Waterloo

Ravine

S
E ——— W

Map of the farm buildings, orchard and garden of La Haye Sainte drawn in the 1830s – NB the north/south orientation is reversed. The double line across the road indicates the barricade thrown up in that position; the 'ravine' is the feature normally called the 'sandpit'. From the many excellent fire positions in the orchard and buildings the rifles of the garrison could inflict casualties far beyond the range of the common musket. The Baker rifle was fairly accurate out to 200 yards, and in the hands of a skilled rifleman could be lethal at 300 – about the maximum effective battle range of a short-barrelled modern military rifle. (Author's collection)

upon the barn, in a more united position, in order to continue the defence …

'Colonel von Klencke now came to our assistance with the Lüneburg Battalion [Hanoverian Army infantry]. We immediately made a counter-attack, and had already made the enemy give way when I perceived a strong line of cuirassiers form up in front of the orchard; at the same time Captain Meyer came to me and reported that the enemy had surrounded the rear garden, and it was not possible to hold it longer. I gave him orders to fall back into the buildings and assist in their defence. Convinced of the great danger which threatened us from the cuirassiers … I called to my men, who were mixed with the newly arrived Hanoverians, to assemble round me, as I intended retiring into the barn. The number of [Lüneburgers] exceeded … that of my men, and … seeing the cuirassiers in the open field [the Luneburgers] imagined that their only chance of safety lay in gaining the main position of the army, [to which they hurriedly withdrew]. … In this effort a part succeeded [sweeping Baring and some of his men along with them] … The farmhouse itself was still defended by Lieutenants Groeme and Carey, and Ensign Frank. The English Dragoon Guards now came up, beat back the cuirassiers, fell upon the [French] infantry … and nearly cut them to pieces.' [Baring then returned to the farm.]

'In this first attack I lost a considerable number of men … On my requisition for support, Captains von Gilsa and Marschalck were sent to me with their companies of the 1st Light Battalion. To these, and a part of my own battalion, I gave the defence of the garden, leaving the buildings to the three officers who had already so bravely defended them; I did not re-occupy the orchard.

'About half an hour's respite was now given us by the enemy, and we employed the time in preparing ourselves against a new attack. This followed in the same force as before: namely, from two sides by two close columns, which, with the greatest rapidity, nearly surrounded us and, despising danger, fought with a degree of courage which I had never before witnessed in Frenchmen. Favoured by their advancing in masses, every bullet of ours hit, and seldom were the effects limited to one assailant. This did not, however, prevent them from throwing themselves against the walls, and endeavouring to wrest the weapons from the hands of my men through the loopholes. Many lives were sacrificed to the defence of the doors and gates; the most obstinate contest was carried on where the gate was missing [having been burned for firewood by other troops the previous night], and where the enemy seemed determined to enter. On this spot seventeen Frenchmen already lay dead, and their bodies served as a protection to those who pressed after them …

'Meantime four lines of French cavalry had formed on the right front of the farm … and it was clear to me that their intention was to attack the

Private, 1st Hussars, 1815

A

1: Corporal, 1st Light Dragoons, marching order, 1815
2: Officer, 2nd Light Dragoons, summer dress, 1815

B

LIGHT INFANTRY, 1813
1: Officer,1st Light Battalion
2: Corporal, 2nd Light Battalion
3: Sharpshooter, 5th Line Battalion

C

MUSICIANS, 1815
1: Serpent, line battalion band
2: Bugler, light company, line battalion
3: Bugler, 2nd Light Battalion
4: Bass drum, 2nd Line Battalion
5: Percussion, 1st Light Battalion

LINE BATTALIONS, 1813-15
1: Sergeant-major, line bn., Belgium
2: Colour-sergeant, Light Coy., 7th Line Bn.,Sicily
3: Lt., Grenadier Coy., 5th Line Bn., Belgium

1
2
3

LINE BATTALIONS 1813-15
1: Private, 5th Line Bn., 1815
2: Surgeon, 5th Line Bn., 1813
3: Corporal, centre coy., 1st Line Bn.

F

Driver, 4th Foot Battery KGA, 1815

1

2

6

7

4

5

3

H

squares of our division ... This was a critical moment, for what would be our fate if they succeeded? As they advanced past the farm towards the [main] position I brought all possible fire to bear upon them; many men and horses were overthrown, but they were not discouraged ... They advanced with the greatest intrepidity, and attacked the infantry ... When the [enemy] cavalry retired, the infantry also gave up their fruitless attack and fell back ... Our loss on this occasion was not so great as from the first attack ...

'Our first care was to make good the damage which had been sustained; my greatest anxiety was respecting the ammunition, which I found, in consequence of our continuous firing, had been reduced by more than one-half [i.e. each man had now less than 30 rounds]. I immediately sent an officer back with this account, and requested ammunition, which was promised. About an hour had thus passed when I saw the enemy's columns again advancing on the farm; I sent another officer back to the [main] position with this intelligence, and repeated the request for ammunition.

'Our small position was soon attacked again with the same fury, and defended with the same courage as before. Captain von Wurmb was sent to my assistance with the skirmishers of the 5th Line Battalion, and I placed them in the courtyard; but welcome as this reinforcement was, it could not compensate for the want of ammunition, which every moment increased, so that after half an hour more of uninterrupted fighting I sent off an officer with the same request.

'This was as fruitless as the other two applications; however, two hundred Nassau troops were sent to me. The principal contest was now carried on at the open entrance to the barn; at length the enemy, not being able to succeed by open force, resorted to the expedient of setting the place on fire, and soon a thick smoke was seen rising from the barn ... Luckily the Nassau troops carried large field cooking kettles ... and filling the kettles with water, they carried them ... to the fire. My men did the same, and soon not one of the Nassauers was left with his kettle, and the fire was thus luckily extinguished ...

'It would be injustice to a skirmisher named Frederick Lindau if I did not mention him. Bleeding from two wounds in the head ... he stood at the small back barn door, and from thence defended the main entrance to his front. I told him to go back, as the cloth about his head was not sufficient to stop the strong flow of blood; he ... answered that "he would be a scoundrel that deserted you so long as his head is on his shoulders". [This was the Lindau whose account of the fighting at Albuhera and Salamanca is recorded in MAA 338.] This attack may have lasted about an hour and a half before the French, tired from their fruitless efforts, again fell back. ...

'Imagine what must have been my feelings, therefore, when, on counting the cartridges, I found that on an average there were no more than three to four for each man ... I was not capable of sustaining another attack in the present condition ...

'The enemy gave me no time for thought; they attacked with renewed fury. The contest commenced at the barn, which they again succeeded in setting on fire. It was extinguished, luckily, in the same manner as before. Every shot that was now fired increased my uneasiness and anxiety. I sent again to the rear with the positive statement that I must

Major George Baring (1773-1848) commanded the 2nd Light Bn and attached troops who formed the garrison of La Haye Sainte. Their heroic defence of the farm which anchored Wellington's centre might have continued beyond the crisis of the battle had the defenders not run out of ammunition for their rifles. Baring made much of his repeated requests for ammunition in his account of the fight for La Haye Sainte, but has since been criticised for failing to ensure that reserve ammunition was brought up to the position before the battle commenced. He later had a distinguished career in the Hanoverian Army. (Author's drawing after anonymous portrait)

and would leave the place if no ammunition was sent to me. This was also without effect.

'Our fire gradually diminished, and in the same proportion did our perplexity increase; already I heard many voices calling out for ammunition, adding "We will readily stand by you, but we must have the means of defending ourselves!" Even the officers, who, during the whole day, had shown the greatest courage, represented to me the impossibility of holding the post under such circumstances. The enemy, who all too soon observed our difficulties, now boldly broke in one of the doors; however, as only a few could come in at a time, these were instantly bayoneted, and those behind them hesitated to follow. They now climbed up on the roof and walls, from which my unfortunate men were easy targets; at the same time they pressed in through the open barn, which could no longer be defended ... I gave the order to retire through the house into the garden ...

'As I was now fully convinced, and the officers agreed with me, that the garden could not be held when the enemy were in possession of the

Adolph Northen's spirited painting of the fighting at La Haye Sainte, executed in the 1850s. It depicts Maj Baring – at centre on horseback, wearing a cocked hat – directing the defence of the farm buildings. The viewpoint is west to east; to the right is the burning barn, and to the left the farmhouse. Beyond the group of figures in the courtyard can be seen the main entrance, with a dovecote above, and the pigsties, from which figures are seen hurling tiles at the French. Amongst the many uniforms visible are those of the 2nd Light Bn and the

(continued opposite)

dwelling house, I made the men retire singly to the main position ... The men who had been sent to me from other regiments I allowed to return, and with the weak remnant of my own battalion I attached myself to two companies of the 1st Light Battalion, which ... occupied the hollow lane behind the farm. Although we could not fire a shot, we helped to increase the numbers ...

'Out of nearly four hundred men with whom I began the battle, only forty-two remained effective. Whomever I asked after, the answer was "killed" or "wounded". I freely confess that tears came to my eyes at this sad news, and many bitter feelings seized upon me.' [The interior of La Haye Sainte at this time was described by a British captive as 'completely destroyed, nothing but the rafters and props remaining. The floor ... was strewed with the bodies of German Infantry and French Tirailleurs. A Major in green lay by the door. The carnage had been very great in this place.'] After the defeat of the French Baring slept upon the battlefield, to awake to a scene that appalled him:

'But I will pass over in silence the scene which the field of battle now presented, with all its misery and grief. We buried our dead friends and comrades; amongst the rest Colonel von Ompteda, the commander of the Brigade, and many brave men. After some food was cooked and the men had, in some measure, refreshed themselves, we broke up from the field to follow the enemy.'

Thus was La Haye Sainte held to the last round and almost to the last man. Had rifle ammunition been brought up to Baring's men they would doubtless have held the position to the end of the battle. It was later shown that rifle ammunition was available, but that the requests for it never got through.

The Line Battalions

As the survivors of the 2nd Light were evacuating the farm soon after 6 o'clock, Sir Charles Alten, their divisional commander, ordered Col von Ompteda to send forward the 5th Line Battalion to attack the French infantry pursuing Baring and his men, and to give them covering fire. Von Ompteda, who had noticed French cavalry nearby through the rolling clouds of gunsmoke, protested the order, but was told to obey his general by the Prince of Orange, who had overheard the exchange. The prince was notorious for his bad battlefield decisions, but on this occasion Alten must clearly bear the main blame. Pausing only to commend his two teenage nephews to the care of Von Linsingen, the battalion commander, Von Ompteda mounted his horse, ordered the 5th into line (they had been formed in square to fight cavalry) and, at their head, advanced on the French infantry, giving them a volley and charging

Field-Marshal Gebhard von Blücher, Prince of Wahlstadt (1742-1819), co-victor at the battle of Waterloo. A cavalryman for most of his life, he fought against the French in 1793 and 1806, and in 1813 took command in Silesia before defeating Napoleon at Leipzig. In command of the Prussian army in 1815, he suffered a defeat at Ligny (and was trapped under his fallen horse); but with the aid of his superb chief-of-staff Von Gneisenau he was able to extricate his forces, regroup them, and march to the aid of Wellington on 18 June. The arrival of his troops on the field of Waterloo turned a French setback into a rout. He rejoiced in the nickname of *Alte Vorwärts* ('Old Forwards') from his habit of attacking. (Author's collection)

with the bayonet. The enemy infantry ran, but riding out of the mists of smoke came a regiment of cuirassiers. They charged into the flank and rear of the 5th Line who, with their muskets unloaded, were cut to pieces. Von Ompteda was among those killed, a colour of the battalion was lost, and only 19 men (including young Christian and Louis von Ompteda) escaped back to the Anglo-Dutch line, pursued by the jubilant French cavalry. These latter first came under fire from the riflemen of the 1st Light Battalion and were then charged by the KGL 3rd Hussars, who locked into the cuirassiers for a furious quarter-hour of swordplay until being obliged to withdraw by the arrival of a body of French lancers.

An officer of the 5th Line witnessed the death of Col von Ompteda: 'I saw that the French had their muskets pointing at the Colonel, but they did not fire. The officers struck the men's barrels up with their swords. They seemed astonished at the extraordinary calm approach of the solitary horseman whose white plume showed him to be an officer of high rank. He soon reached the enemy line of infantry before the [La Haye Sainte] garden hedge. He jumped in, and I clearly saw his sword blows smite the shakos off. The nearest French officer looked on with admiration without attempting to check the attack.' Later the observer saw Von Ompteda '... sink from his horse and vanish.'

While the fight for the central bastion of La Haye Sainte had raged, a succession of French infantry and cavalry attacks had broken against the Anglo-Dutch line on either side of the farm. During one of these the 8th Line Battalion had also been caught in the act of charging in line by enemy cuirassiers. Like the 5th later in the day, the 8th had been cut down, losing their King's Colour and so many men that, although they rallied, they were ineffective as a unit for the rest of the battle, the survivors being drawn up into a square under the command of one of their surviving officers.

The units of the King's German Legion in the centre of Wellington's line had seen their share of hard fighting; now it was the turn of those on the right. With the Prussians applying pressure on his right flank, Napoleon issued orders to send in his Imperial Guard between Hougoumont and La Haye Sainte. At about 7pm, 14 battalions of Grenadiers and Chasseurs of the Guard advanced under the leadership of Marshal Ney. Two columns advancing in echelon got right up to the Anglo-Dutch line before they were checked by the devastating fire of Wellington's artillery; thrown into confusion, they gave way under a succession of murderous musket volleys, and began to fall back. The spectacle of the Imperial Guard in retreat was too much for Napoleon's men to bear; as the Allies pressed forward from both north and east the fainter-hearted among the French began to leave the field.

Wellington ordered his line to advance, and with it, on the right, went Du Plat's 1st KGL Brigade and Maj Kuhlmann's KGA horse battery. Du Plat's men had stood in column without taking part in the battle until about 4pm, when they were moved up around Hougoumont and became involved in the fighting for that place. Formed in squares the 1st, 3rd and 4th Line Battalions beat off an attack by enemy cavalry, while the 2nd Line pressed on towards Hougoumont, driving the enemy from its garden. The brigade now advanced past the blazing manor, capturing a battery of French guns but suffering heavy losses including Col du Plat, killed at the head of his men.

At the side of the 1st KGL Brigade was a brigade of Hanoverian Landwehr or militia commanded by Col Hugh Halkett of the KGL 7th Line Battalion. Under Halkett's direction the Osnabrück Battalion attacked and broke a square of the Imperial Guard, while he rode forward and captured the French brigade commander, Gen Cambronne, dragging him into captivity by the aiguilette cords on his coat.

In the general advance the 2nd Light Dragoons of the KGL made a charge upon a large body of enemy cavalry. This turned into a mêlée which at first went against the 2nd, but they managed to recover the situation and put the enemy to flight, capturing a gun in the process. Also in the pursuit of the retreating French were the KGL 1st Hussars, now accompanied by the redoubtable Maj George Baring.

Under pressure from both the Anglo-Dutch line and the Prussian forces who, by early evening, were present in great and increasing numbers, the French retreat dissolved into a rout. His troops exhausted, Wellington handed over the pursuit to Blücher, and in the respite that followed the cost of the battle began to be reckoned. To this day controversy exists as to the numbers of casualties among the armies which fought at Waterloo. One source gives the French losses as over 35,000 men, and Wellington's casualties as about 16,000. Other estimates vary widely. In the King's German Legion the casualty list amounted to 1,726 killed, wounded and missing from the total of 7,004 officers and men on the muster rolls at the time of the battle.

THE DISBANDING OF THE LEGION

The Allied armies pursued the French to Paris. The latter made no cohesive stand after the battle at Mont St Jean, and advance elements of the pursuing Prussian cavalry crossed the frontier into France on the night of 18 June. The battle of Waterloo, as the British subsequently named it, swept Napoleon out of power and finally into lifelong exile on bleak St Helena. (The French more properly called the battle 'Mont St Jean', while the Prussians preferred 'La Belle Alliance', after the aptly named inn where Blücher and Wellington met in their moment of victory.) The

Tackmann print of an officer of the 1st Cavalry Regt (Life Guard Cuirassiers) of the Hanoverian Army, post-1816. This regiment retained the traditions of the 1st Dragoons, KGL, including the battle honours awarded for 'Peninsula', 'Garcia Hernandez' and 'Waterloo'. By 1914 this unit had evolved into the 13th King's Uhlan Regt (1st Hanoverian) of the Imperial German Army. (Anne S.K.Brown Collection)

BELOW **A splendid Tackmann print of a trumpeter of the Guard Hussar Regt, Hanoverian Army, post-1816. The Guard Hussars took over the traditions and battle honours of the KGL 1st Hussars including 'Peninsula', 'El Bodon' and 'Waterloo'. Eventually the unit evolved into Queen Wilhelmina of the Netherlands' Hussar Regt (Hanoverian) No.15 as part of the Prussian-dominated Imperial German Army. The trumpeter is distinguished by a red dolman, pelisse and plume, and a white horse. The hussars in the background have the red facings of the old KGL 1st Hussars. (Anne S.K.Brown Collection)**

Bourbon Louis XVIII was re-installed on the throne of France; the French armies withdrew to the river Loire, while the Allies occupied Paris.

With the achievement of final victory the days of the King's German Legion were numbered. By proclamation of the Prince Regent, dated 24 December 1815, the units of the KGL were ordered to march home to Hanover, there to be disbanded. Those with Wellington's Army of the Netherlands set off from Paris to various chosen destinations in their homeland, and were disbanded by 24 February 1816; the Foreign Veteran Battalion was also disbanded on that date. The 6th and 7th Line Battalions, with the 3rd Foot Battery, received the Prince Regent's order in Italy. Embarking at Genoa, they arrived in the Ems at the end of April and were disbanded on 24 May 1816. The King's German Legion was no more. In the years since 1803 over 28,000 men had served Britain in its ranks, of which 5,848 lost their lives.

Perhaps the best epitaph to the Legion was written in 1816. It referred, in part, to the 'ever memorable campaigns, in which the

Shako of Jäger Battalion No.10 (Hanoverian) of the Imperial German Army, c.1914; note the battle honours 'Waterloo', 'Peninsula' and 'Venta del Pozo' won by the Light battalions of the KGL. (Courtesy Ken Dunn)

OPPOSITE **Another Tackmann print depicting an officer of the 3rd Cavalry Regt (Duke of Cambridge's Hussars) of the Hanoverian Army, post-1816. This unit retained the traditions of the KGL 3rd Hussars, including the battle honours 'Peninsula', 'Waterloo' and 'Göhrde'. The hussar uniform has yellow facings and silver lace, the battle honours are worn on the fur cap, and the sabretasche carries the cypher of King George IV (1820-1830). In the Imperial German Army this unit's lineage was maintained by the 9th Dragoon Regt (1st Hanoverian); its colonel was King Charles I of Rumania. (Anne S.K.Brown Collection)**

RIGHT **Print by Tackmann depicting an officer of the 2nd or Osnabrück Hussars, Hanoverian Army, which continued the traditions of the KGL 2nd Hussars, including white uniform facings and their battle honours 'Peninsula' and 'Barossa'. By 1914 this unit had also been absorbed into the Imperial German Army's Queen Wilhelmina of the Netherlands' Hussar Regt (Hanoverian) No.15. Note that at the time depicted Hanoverian units wore their battle honours on scrolls on their caps. (Anne S.K.Brown Collection)**

39

RIGHT **Private soldier of the Grenadier Guard Regt, Hanoverian Army, post-1816. Tackmann's print shows the summer dress of the time, which strongly resembles that of a soldier of the British Grenadier Guards. Note his cap plate with grenade badge, blue wings (still apparently bearing a fringe above and below), plain white lace, Royal blue facings, and British pattern musket. (Anne S.K.Brown Collection)**

BELOW **Pattern 1910 Imperial German Army field grey tunic (and shoulder strap detail) of a subaltern officer of Prince Albert of Prussia's Fusilier Regt (Hanoverian) No.73, c.1914. The most striking feature is the gold-on-bright-blue 'GIBRALTAR' cuff-title awarded in the late 18th century to the 3rd, 5th and 6th Infantry Regiments of the Hanoverian Army for service to the British monarchy in that much-besieged fortress. In the First World War this cuff-title was also worn by Von Voights-Rhetz Infantry Regt (3rd Hanoverian) No.79 and Jäger Battalion No.10 (Hanoverian). The uniform piping is red, the buttons and cypher gilt, the shoulder strap silver braid with black thread chevrons on white underlay. (Courtesy Ken Dunn)**

Legion bore their share, while forming part of the British Army in the Peninsula. In the fields of Talavera, Salamanca and Vittoria, rendered immortal by the combined exertions of British and German valour, they have laid the imperishable foundations of a renown [to which] the Battle of Waterloo was alone capable of adding an increased splendour.'

* * *

Many officers and men of the disbanded units went on to serve with regiments of the Hanoverian Army, taking with them the battle honours they had won when the traditions of the KGL were absorbed by the Hanoverian units. The colours of the regiments and battalions of the Legion were laid up in the garrison church in Osnabrück.

In 1867 Prussia annexed Hanover and disbanded the Hanoverian Army; but on 24 January 1899 the Prussian emperor issued an order that the traditions of the units of the King's German Legion were once more to be taken up by the Hanoverian units of the Imperial German Army. The lineages of the former KGL and Hanoverian Army units at the outbreak of the Great War were as follows:

Lineage of The King's German Legion post-1816

KGL units 1815	Hanoverian Army post-1816	Imperial German Army 1914
1st Light Dragoons	Garde-Reiter-Reg	Königs-Ulanen-Regt (1. Hannoversches) Nr.13
2nd Light Dragoons	2 or Leib-Reiter-Regt	Ulanen-Regt Nr.14 (2. Hannoversches)
1st Hussars	1 or Garde-Husaren-Regt	Husaren-Regt Königin Wilhelmina von der Niederlande (Hannoversches) Nr.15
2nd Hussars	2 or Osnabrücksches Husaren-Regt	
3rd Hussars	3 or Göttingensches Husaren-Regt	Dragoner-Regt König Carl I von Rumanien (1. Hannoversches) Nr.9
1st Light Bn	Garde-Jäger-Bataillon	Jäger-Bataillon No.10 (Hannoversches)
2nd Light Bn		
3rd Line Bn	2. Garde-Bataillon	
4th Line Bn		
1st Line Bn	1. Grenadier-Garde-Bataillon	Fusilier-Regt Prinz Albert von Preussen (Hannoversches) Nr.73
2nd Line Bn		
5th Line Bn	(Hannoversches) 3. Garde-Bataillon	
8th Line Bn		
6th Line Bn	Landwehr-Bataillone Emden, Leer and Aurich	
7th Line Bn		

LEFT **Feldwebel (senior sergeant) of the Guard Jäger Battalion of the Hanoverian Army, post-1816, by Tackmann. This unit carried on the traditions of both the KGL Light battalions and bore the battle honours 'Peninsula', 'Waterloo' and 'Venta del Pozo'; the jacket is dark green with black facings and white trim. By 1914 this lineage had passed down to Jäger Battalion No.10 (Hanoverian) in the Imperial German Army. (Anne S.K.Brown Collection)**

UNIFORMS 1812-1816

The dress and insignia of the KGL changed little over the first decade of its existence. But when, in February 1811, the illness (thought to be madness) of King George III brought about the passing of the Regency Act, changes in uniform became inevitable.

The king's eldest son was George, Prince of Wales, and his lifestyle had been a cause for concern to king and Parliament for many years. Amongst his many self-indulgences was that of dandyism, imagining himself an authority on sartorial elegance, adorning his portly frame with costumes expensive enough for 'the first gentleman of Europe', and consorting with the most famous dandies of the day. He may have known little of soldiering, but he considered himself an expert on military fashion.

Shortly after the Prince became Regent his brother the Duke of York (whom the nursery rhyme described marching his 10,000 men 'to the top of the hill' and down again) was reinstated as Commander-in-Chief, a position he had been forced to resign in 1809 after a scandal involving the sale of commissions by his mistress. Under the chairmanship of yet another royal brother, the Duke of Cumberland, a board of general officers was set up to report on new clothing and equipment for the cavalry, the Prince Regent taking a keen interest in its deliberations. Before the year was out orders had been issued for new uniforms for officers, and in the new year of 1812 new patterns for the rank and file were 'sealed'. Little of this tinkering was of any practical value.

There were extensive changes for the heavy cavalry and for the Light Dragoons, who were ordered to wear shakos similar to those of the French, and jackets cut in the style of Polish lancers. This was to be the type of uniform adopted by the two Dragoon regiments of the KGL when they were converted to Light Dragoons in December 1813. From this date the three original Light Dragoon regiments of the Legion were officially styled 'Hussars', a title they had used unofficially for years; as they had also long worn hussar uniform their dress was not altered.

Changes of dress followed for other arms. In December 1811 a new shako was ordered for officers and men of the infantry of the line and foot artillery. Called the 'Belgique', later 'Waterloo' or 'Wellington' shako, it had a false front $8\frac{1}{2}$ins in height on which was set a shield-shaped plate. Tufts, plumes and cockades were as before but were placed on the left of the cap, which was festooned across the front with a plaited cord and tassels. (It may have been practice in the KGL for grenadiers to wear the cords from their bearskin caps around the front and back of this shako; at least one sketch shows this.) Some light infantry units retained the former 'stovepipe' shako, but in 1814 all were ordered to wear a bugle-horn badge and regimental number on their shakos in place of any other badge. Light infantry of the KGL appear only to have worn the bugle-horn.

Not all the uniform changes emanating from the board were pointless. The grey trousers authorised in August 1811 were a great improvement on the white netherwear previously issued. From 1811 infantry officers were ordered to put aside their dark blue greatcoats and to take into use grey coats of the same shade as their men. They were also ordered to wear jackets and grey trousers, similar in cut to those now

A centre company officer of a Line battalion of the KGL, c.1815. Another of the series of line-and-wash drawings by Capt Count Castell, showing a uniform according exactly with the regulations of the time, with gold lace and dark blue facings. He wears the single epaulette of a junior officer, and carries the 1796 pattern infantry sword, a straight-bladed weapon with a shell-and-bar guard. (Author's collection)

worn by their men; from now on the long-tailed coat and cocked hat were only worn in levée dress.

In 1813 the rank of colour-sergeant was introduced for 'one sergeant in each company of every regiment of infantry', the original order stating that a badge depicting a regimental colour and crossed swords was to be worn by these non-commissioned officers. This was later changed to a badge with a Union flag, crossed swords and a crown, all over a single chevron. (The surviving coat upon which Plates E2 and H4 are based carries the badge of rank of the rare, earlier pattern.)

The meddling of the Regent in the dress of his soldiers continued, resulting in some showy and impractical costumes after the peace of 1815, but the KGL had been disbanded before their issue.

The preserved uniforms

Several KGL uniforms have survived to our day preserved in museums in northern Germany, particularly the Bomann Museum at Celle. Of special interest are a number of rank-and-file red coats, all to sergeants. These are the only Napoleonic period sergeant's-quality red coats of the Line (as opposed to one or two militia examples) known to be in existence. They include one to a colour-sergeant of the light company of the 7th Line Battalion, one to a sergeant of the grenadier company of the 4th Line, and one to a sergeant of a battalion company of the same unit. All have the plain white lace which was laid down for sergeants' coats, but otherwise the examples depart from regulations, displaying a number of interesting regimental variations. These will be found illustrated in the colour plates of this volume and MAA 338.

Other preserved KGL uniforms include examples to the cavalry and the artillery. Most of the preserved headdress is of the 'Belgique' pattern which, like the uniforms, was the last clothing being worn by the officers and sergeants who donated these items after the disbanding of the Legion. Together these relics form one of the most important collections of British military uniform of the Napoleonic Wars.

Weapons and equipment

There was little change in the weapons of the KGL over this period, other than the re-arming of the Dragoon regiments with the swords and carbines of light cavalry after their conversion to Light Dragoons.

Equipment also changed little. The decision to provide tentage for the infantry from 1813 resulted in the issue of tinplate camp kettles, mess tins and billhooks which were carried by the men in order to make room on unit transport for the tents. The camp kettles shown in a sketch of soldiers of the 5th Line Battalion are of a square pattern. They were usually carried in a canvas bag strapped to the top of the knapsack. In the KGL blankets/greatcoats were not rolled and strapped above the knapsack as in the usual British practice, but folded and strapped to its outer flap.

THE PLATES

A: Private, 1st Hussars, 1815

Depicted in marching order, our subject is mounted on a troop horse which has the cropped 'nag-tail' of the period. The ears of these unfortunate animals were also cropped to provide a fashionable appearance. The colourful shabraques – saddlecloths – which bore regimental devices were not put on the horse in marching order, the only visible distinguishing marks being those on the valise worn behind the saddle. In the case of the cavalry of the Legion these bore the initials 'KGL.' on the 'off' or right side, and the regimental initials on the 'near' or left (see Plate H6 and H7); it was often the

practice to include the troop number also. A folded blanket is worn beneath our subject's 1805 pattern light cavalry saddle, a cloak is strapped over the pistol holsters in front of it, and a sheepskin cover is secured over it. The bridle is the 1812 light cavalry pattern. Note the breast straps and crupper securing the saddle front and rear, and the 'waterdeck' oilskin sheet wrapped around the valise.

The soldier wears the hussar fur cap of the period, which by then had chinscales for added protection. Note his side-plaits and hussar moustaches. The troopers of the 1st Hussars of the KGL were distinguished by their red facings and yellow lace, the black fur trim to their pelisses, and their blue overalls with red stripes. They were armed with the 1796 pattern light cavalry sabre, a carbine and pistols. Note the plain sabretasche worn by cavalry rank-and-file. In the background flies a camp colour of the KGL 1st Hussars.

B1: Corporal, 1st Light Dragoons, marching order, 1815

Some time elapsed before the Dragoons of the KGL were uniformed, armed and equipped as Light Dragoons. In the interim an odd mixture of dress was worn, but by the time of Waterloo their appearance conformed to regulations. The corporal's horse has an 1812 pattern light cavalry bridle, which was distinguished by its rosettes and crossed face-straps. Here again the blue shabraque, ornamented with regimental devices, was not worn. His saddle is the light cavalry pattern with holsters, to which are strapped a rolled cloak, valise, waterdeck and sheepskin cover. His carbine is attached to his saddle by means of a 'boot', and his valise bears the initials of his regiment and troop on the nearside (the legend 'KGL.' appearing on the offside).

In the field, his shako insignia is obscured by an oilskin cover; these included a band of lace, cap lines and roundel, all in yellow, the national cockade and a white-over-red tuft. The lapels of his jacket are buttoned over so as not to display the red facings beneath, another marching order expedient. His equipment includes a pouch belt with swivel and clip for attachment to the carbine, a pouch in rear for 20 carbine/pistol cartridges, a buckle in rear for adjustment, and a tab to secure the belt to the epaulette button. His sword belt has slings for his 1796 pattern light cavalry sabre and his sabretasche. He carries a haversack and a canteen (water bottle) slung high behind his left hip.

B2: Officer, 2nd Light Dragoons, summer dress, 1815

This 'summer dress' was a form of undress. His jacket is worn open, with the facings buttoned back, over a white waistcoat and overalls. A fur undress cap is decorated with lace and tassel, and the girdle is worn under the jacket. This

A water-colour sketch by an unknown German artist of an officer of the 1st Hussars, c.1815. The colours and facings of his uniform are as for the private depicted in Plate A, but the quality is of a much higher order, lavishly decorated with gold lace.

Like so many of the paintings of the officers and men of the KGL this study was probably painted many years after their disbandment. Very few contemporary studies exist, those that do often having anomalies or puzzling captions. (Bomann Museum, Celle)

was one of a number of orders of dress for officers in this regiment, including 'common drill order', 'marching order' and 'full dress'.

C: LIGHT INFANTRY, 1813

C1: Officer, 1st Light Battalion, campaign dress
The uniform worn by officers of the 1st Light differed considerably from that worn in the 2nd Light Battalion. The jacket of the 1st contrasted especially with the dolman jacket of the 2nd. Note our subject's shako with square-cut peak, black cords and distinctive plume. Note also his sabre, black pouch belt with whistle, black sword belt, black facings, and the black 'strapping' to his overalls.

C2: Corporal, 2nd Light Battalion
The greatcoats worn by the rank and file of the KGL were made up without the cape worn by other British troops. Our corporal's headdress is the standard light infantry shako worn without a peak and decorated to resemble a mirleton cap. Equipment in the KGL Light battalions was made of black leather or canvas, and included at this time a 60-round pouch and pouch belt with powder horn; a waist belt with 'ball-bag' and sword-bayonet; a 'Trotter' frame knapsack; a haversack, and a canteen. The latter were invariably marked with regimental, battalion and company initials as shown. Note our subject's badge of rank and bugle-horn shako badge.

By this time also the British-made Baker rifle, shown here, had become available in considerable numbers. Made in .62in calibre, the rifle fired a ball of 20 to 22 to the pound, according to whether a patched ball or a cartridge was used. For patched ball shooting four drams of powder were poured into the barrel from the powder horn, but six drams were contained in cartridges when the rifle was used as a musket. Unlike the India pattern musket, whose .75in bore could accept smaller calibre ammunition at a pinch, the bore of the Baker rifle was too small to accept British musket, carbine or pistol ammunition; nor would it accept French ammunition. The disastrous consequences of this design fault at La Haye Sainte are described in the text.

C3: 'Sharpshooter', 5th Line Battalion
This soldier of the sharpshooter platoon of his battalion's Light Company – note the shoulder wings – is also armed with a Baker rifle, and his equipment is identical to that of C2 but made of whitened buff leather. His 'Belgique' shako is protected by an oilskin cover which has a flap that can be let down to protect the neck and ears; chinstraps made of leather or ribbon were widely used in the KGL. Our subject carries a 'Trotter' frame knapsack to which are strapped a greatcoat, a blanket and a camp kettle in its canvas bag. Note the regimental markings on his canteen and pack flap.

Capt Count Castell's drawing of an officer of the 2nd Light Dragoons, c.1815. The degree of accuracy of this line-and-wash study may by gauged by comparing the plume and plume-holder on the subject's shako with the details on Plate H2. Buttons and lace are in silver/white metal except for the gold cap lines, and the pouch belt and girdle of red leather and gold lace; sword belt and slings are of black leather. (Author's collection)

D: MUSICIANS, 1815
In the British Army, in addition to the soldiers officially employed as company drummers and buglers (and therefore carried on the establishment and pay rolls of regiments), extra musicians were hired to make up regimental bands of music. Paid for by regimental funds or officers' subscriptions, they were richly dressed and led by bandmasters who were also privately engaged. Contemporary accounts praise the high standard of the bands of the KGL, who performed the music of their homeland in traditional style.

D1: Serpent player of a Line battalion band
An instrument made of wood and leather, the serpent was difficult to play because of the widely spaced notes. Our subject is dressed in much the same manner as a bandsman of the Foot Guards, with a gold-laced coat, wings and shako cords. Note his bandsman's 'scimitar'.

LEFT **A Castell line-and-wash drawing of a 'skirmisher' (sharpshooter?) of a Line battalion of the KGL, c.1815. Here again Castell has drawn the tufts of the wings but not the red wings themselves. He shows a green shako tuft and white cords; the red jacket has dark blue facings, and the equipment for the Baker rifle is of whitened buff leather. The picker and brush hang on chains attached to the breast of his jacket. (Author's collection)**

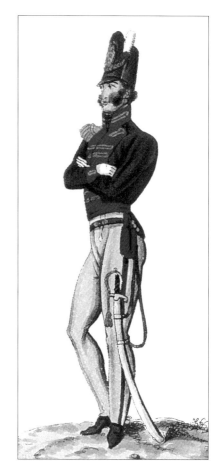

RIGHT **An officer of foot artillery, KGA, c.1815, by Castell. He wears a white-over-red shako plume, and his dark blue jacket is faced scarlet. His grey overalls have a scarlet stripe, his lace is gold, and the sword belt for his sabre is of black leather. Around his waist is the crimson sash that was one of the badges of rank of an officer in the British service. (Author's collection)**

D2: Bugler, Light Company of a Line battalion

His coat is decorated with drummer's lace and he sounds a bugle with a single turn (bugles with two turns, the modern form, were yet to be devised). Note his green shako tuft and cords, also his by-then-obsolete shako badges.

D3: Bugler, 2nd Light Battalion

He plays a 'cor de chasse' or French horn, an instrument more popular in Continental armies than in the British. His red uniform and shako decorations mark him as a bugler, and the cut of his jacket as a member of the 2nd Light Battalion, KGL.

D4: Bass drummer, 2nd Line Battalion band

Dressed in the same style of uniform as D1, he protects his clothing from damage from his drum by a buff leather apron. Bass drums of the time were quite different from those of today, being much longer but smaller in diameter. Note the rows of brass rivets where the wooden shell was joined; and the blazoning on the shell, which includes the Royal cypher and crown, a garland of roses, thistles and shamrock, and a scroll with the battalion title.

D5: Percussionist, 1st Light Battalion band

It was fashionable to employ African percussionists as members of regimental bands. They played drums, cymbals, tambourines, and sometimes an instrument of Austro-Hungarian origin called a *schellenbaum*, a staff upon which hung scores of small bells (termed in English a 'Jingling Johnnie', this was originally copied from the Turks). Called *Janitscharen* in the KGL, and dressed in a style thought to resemble that of the Turkish Janissaries of old, they danced on the march, adding spectacle to the splendour of the music. Note this bandsman's 'Moorish' costume, the black leather and green of which indicate his regiment, and his musician's 'scimitar'. After the battle of Salamanca the 1st Light Battalion fought an action in which their *Janitschar* bass drummer, his drum, and the donkey which carried it were taken prisoner. On the following day the 1st Light were entering Madrid behind their band when they heard the beat of the bass drum joining in with the march the band was playing. Soon afterwards they beheld their drummer, leading the donkey with one hand and beating time with the other as he raced to take his place in the column.

E & F: LINE BATTALIONS, 1813-15

E1: Sergeant-Major of a Line battalion; Belgium

His uniform is that of an officer of the KGL, with the coat cut from scarlet cloth and decorated with gold lace, gilt buttons and officer's-pattern turnback badges. His shako is festooned with gold cord, he wears a scarlet silk sash, and his trousers have a gold stripe on the seams. His shoulder straps are trimmed with gold lace and fringing, and his badge of rank – four chevrons below a crown – is also of gold lace and embroidery. Armed with a 1796 pattern infantry sword, he carries a cane and – just visible – his notebook tucked into his jacket. Note that by this time gaiters were made from the same grey material as trousers.

E2: Colour-Sergeant, Light Company, 7th Line Battalion; Sicily

The 3rd, 4th, 6th, 7th and 8th Line Battalions of the KGL all served for long periods in Sicily, from whence they took part in a number of expeditions including operations to the Gulf of Naples, the Catalonian coast of Spain, Italy, Malta and Corsica. He wears a straw 'round hat' with a light infantry plume, as reportedly worn in the Mediterranean, and his coat is based on a garment surviving in Celle, which has possibly unique padded wings with bugle-horn badges (see H5). His badge of rank is of the first pattern ordered, a regimental colour and swords (see H4) above three chevrons. The latter are made of gold lace. Note his whistle, picker and brush chains, sergeant's sash, and .65in calibre sergeant's carbine.

E3: Lieutenant, Grenadier Company, 5th Line Battalion; Belgium

This is a likeness, taken from his published self-portrait, of Lt Edmund Wheatley, one of a number of Englishmen commissioned into units of the KGL, in his case from 1812 to 1816. He wrote and illustrated a diary of his battles and adventures in Spain, southern France and in the Waterloo campaign, the text and paintings providing a few first-hand details of the dress and equipment of the Legion, as well as a vivid account of life on active service. Wheatley is depicted in the service dress he wore at the battle of Waterloo, and in which he was captured when his unit was cut down by French cavalry. Note the oilskin cover to his 'Belgique' shako, his grenadier officer's wings, his 1803 pattern flank company officer's sword, and his pipe and haversack; all are either mentioned or drawn in his diary. He was at first held prisoner in the burnt-out shell of La Haye Sainte, then marched to the rear and robbed of his valuables and boots. He eventually managed to escape and rejoin his unit after an incredible series of adventures.

F1: Private, 5th Line Battalion, 1813

In Wheatley's diary is a line-and-wash sketch of men of his unit sitting around a fire, cooking and smoking, dressed as this figure. He wears the slate-grey trousers and gaiters that were by then standard fatigue and service dress. They had what was termed 'split falls' fastening in the front, a single pocket on the right, a fob pocket, an adjusting belt at the rear waist, and leather braces to hold them (and the drawers beneath) up. The waistcoat probably started life as a white garment with red collar and cuffs, but Wheatley shows that it soon became a grubby yellow colour. His 'nightcap' has a very German appearance, piped white and sporting a white tassel. Note his stock, and the inverted 'breast' that was meant to show at the collar of the closed jacket.

F2: Surgeon, 5th Line Battalion, 1813

The jacket is based on a surviving example; note its single-breasted cut. All 'staff' coats were supposed to be made this way, but our subject has adopted the facings and turnback badges of the KGL.

F3: Corporal of a centre company, 1st Line Battalion

His appearance shows the details of rank-and-file uniform of the last years of the King's German Legion. Note the tuft,

cockade, regimental button and cords on his shako; note also the plate for the 'Belgique' cap, shown in detail at Plate H3. Tied up over the crown of his shako is its chinstrap. The lace on his coat shows the blue stripe of a Royal regiment, and his badge of rank is made from the same material, forming two chevrons mounted on blue cloth. His uniform is completed by slate-grey trousers and gaiters. The common footwear was still low shoes. Surrounding him are some of the paraphernalia he and his comrades carried, including a 'Trotter' frame knapsack, a canteen, a mess tin with its lid, a camp kettle without its lid, and a billhook.

G: Driver, 4th (Cleeve's) Foot Battery, King's German Artillery, 1815

Guns were towed by teams of six or eight horses, which were 'driven' in the postillion style by men who rode the nearside horse of each pair. The horse depicted is the 'wheeler' of a team; wheelers were the pair of horses nearest to the gun and limber, and their harness included 'breeching' – a broad strap went around the animal's hindquarters to assist in checking the gun when halting or driving downhill. Other harness shown includes the collar, and the traces and pole chain attached to it which connected horse to vehicle. Draught animals in British service had blinkers attached to the cheek straps of their bridles.

Artillery drivers of the time wore a jacked-leather 'Tarleton'-style helmet similar to that worn by the horse artillery, the jacket of the foot artillery, and overalls. Our subject wears a leather and metal 'leg-iron' on his right leg to prevent it being crushed between the horses and the limber-pole. Into his leg-iron he has tucked his driving whip. His equipment includes a sword belt for his artillery hanger, a haversack, and a canteen. His valise is strapped behind his saddle and his cloak in front.

H: COLOUR AND INSIGNIA

H1: Infantry colours of the KGL conformed to the regulations of the time; this is the King's Colour of the 4th Line Battalion, 1806-1816. A silk Union flag 6ft by 6ft 6ins, it has the crown, cartouche and legend, and the usual roses, thistles and shamrock painted upon it. The pike is almost ten feet in length and the colour is secured to the gilt pike head by red and gold cords.

H2: The shako plume of an officer of the 2nd Light Dragoons KGL, 1815. Fitted in a gilt holder, it was made of 'young bear's fur'.

H3: Rank-and-file 'Belgique' shako plate of the 1st Line Battalion KGL, 1813-1816 (see Plate F3). Officers had a similar pattern but of finer quality.

H4 & H5: Arm badge of a colour-sergeant of the 7th Line Battalion, 1815, and detail of his right shoulder 'wing'; see Plate E2. Note the regimental colour on the badge, indicating the rarely seen first pattern. Note also the bugle-horn detail on the wing.

H6 & H7: KGL insignia on the offside of the valise of an officer of the 2nd Light Dragoons, 1815; and regimental insignia on the nearside.

Select Bibliography

ENGLISH LANGUAGE:

History of the King's German Legion, N.Ludlow Beamish FRS (late Major unattached), 2 vols., London, 1832 & 1837

The Wheatley Diary: a Journal and Sketchbook kept during the Peninsular War and the Waterloo campaign, Lieutenant Edmund Wheatley, London 1964

On the Road with Wellington, Lieutenant Augustus Schaumann, London 1924

'The Raising and Organisation of the King's German Legion', LtCol R.E.F.G.North (Retd), *Journal of the Society for Army Historical Research*

'Prisoners, Wanderers and Deserters: Recruiting for the King's German Legion', 1803-1815, Daniel Savage Grey, *Journal of the Society for Army Historical Research*

'Uniforms of 2nd Dragoons, King's German Legion, 1810-1815', Oberstabstartz Dr F. Herrmann, German Army Medical Corps, & Major P.E.Abbott RA, *Journal of the Society for Army Historical Research*

GERMAN LANGUAGE:

Nec Aspera Terrant, Friedrich Schirmer, Leipzig 1937

Diaries of Colonel Christian von Ompteda, 5th Line Battalion; Friedrich Lindau, 2nd Light Battalion; Major George von Coulon, 8th Line Battalion.

The medals of an NCO of the 1st Hussars, KGL: from left to right, the Guelphic Medal, the Military General Service Medal (1793-1814) and the Waterloo Medal. The Guelphic Medal (with a monthly pension of two dollars) was awarded to those NCOs and men of the KGL who distinguished themselves by extraordinary service. Of the 70-odd awards most went to cavalrymen, with the amazing number of 46 medals going to men of the 1st Hussars. The Military General Service Medal was instituted in 1847, only those veterans still living being able to claim them. In all 29 clasps were authorised; the ten shown here are TALAVERA, BUSACO, FUENTES D'ONOR, CIUDAD RODRIGO, SALAMANCA, VITTORIA, PYRENEES, NIVELLE, ORTHES and TOULOUSE. The Waterloo Medal was instituted in 1816 for those who fought on 16-18 June 1815; in addition recipients were credited with two extra years' service to count for pension, promotion and pay. All the medals were of silver. The ribbons were pale blue and white for the Guelphic Medal and crimson with blue edges for the other two. (Author's collection)

COMPANION SERIES FROM OSPREY

CAMPAIGN

Concise, authoritative accounts of history's decisive military encounters. Each 96-page book contains over 90 illustrations including maps, orders of battle, colour plates, and three-dimensional battle maps.

WARRIOR

Definitive analysis of the appearance, weapons, equipment, tactics, character and conditions of service of the individual fighting man throughout history. Each 64-page book includes full-colour uniform studies in close detail, and sectional artwork of the soldier's equipment.

NEW VANGUARD

Comprehensive histories of the design, development and operational use of the world's armoured vehicles and artillery. Each 48-page book contains eight pages of full-colour artwork including a detailed cutaway.

ORDER OF BATTLE

The most detailed information ever published on the units which fought history's great battles. Each 96-page book contains comprehensive organisation diagrams supported by ultra-detailed colour maps. Each title also includes a large fold-out base map.

ELITE

Detailed information on the organisation, appearance and fighting record of the world's most famous military bodies. This series of 64-page books, each containing some 50 photographs and diagrams and 12 full-colour plates, will broaden in scope to cover personalities, significant military techniques, and other aspects of the history of warfare which demand a comprehensive illustrated treatment.

AIRCRAFT OF THE ACES

Focuses exclusively on the elite pilots of major air campaigns, and includes unique interviews with surviving aces sourced specifically for each volume. Each 96-page volume contains up to 40 specially commissioned artworks, unit listings, new scale plans and the best archival photography available.

COMBAT AIRCRAFT

Technical information from the world's leading aviation writers on the century's most significant military aircraft. Each 96-page volume contains up to 40 specially commissioned artworks, unit listings, new scale plans and the best archival photography available.